The
Love
— AS A —
WAY OF LIFE

DEVOTIONAL

GARY CHAPMAN
AND ELISA STANFORD

The
LOVE
— AS A —
WAY OF LIFE

DEVOTIONAL

WATERBROOK
PRESS

THE LOVE AS A WAY OF LIFE DEVOTIONAL
PUBLISHED BY WATERBROOK PRESS
12265 Oracle Boulevard, Suite 200
Colorado Springs, Colorado 80921
A division of Random House Inc.

All Scripture quotations, unless otherwise indicated, are taken from the Holy Bible, New International Version®. NIV®. Copyright © 1973, 1978, 1984 by International Bible Society. Used by permission of Zondervan Publishing House. All rights reserved. Scripture quotations marked (MSG) are taken from The Message by Eugene H. Peterson. Copyright © 1993, 1994, 1995, 1996, 2000, 2001, 2002. Used by permission of NavPress Publishing Group. All rights reserved. Scripture quotations marked (NASB) are taken from the New American Standard Bible®. © Copyright The Lockman Foundation 1960, 1962, 1963, 1968, 1971, 1972, 1973, 1975, 1977, 1995. Used by permission. (www.Lockman.org). Scripture quotations marked (NKJV) are taken from the New King James Version®. Copyright © 1982 by Thomas Nelson Inc. Used by permission. All rights reserved.

Italics in Scripture quotations reflect the author's added emphasis.

The author has made every effort to ensure the accuracy of the stories and anecdotes in this book. In some instances, names and identifying details have been changed to protect the privacy of the person or persons involved.

ISBN 978-0-30744-469-1

Published in the United States by WaterBrook Multnomah, an imprint of The Doubleday Publishing Group, a division of Random House Inc., New York.

WATERBROOK and its deer colophon are registered trademarks of Random House Inc.

Library of Congress Cataloging-in-Publication Data
Chapman, Gary D., 1938–
    The love as a way of life devotional : a 90-day adventure that makes love a daily habit / Gary Chapman and Elisa Stanford.—1st ed.
       p. cm.
    Includes bibliographical references.
    ISBN 978-0-30744-469-1
    1. Love—Religious aspects—Christianity—Prayers and devotions. 2. Devotional calendars.
I. Stanford, Elisa. II. Title.
    BV4639.C423 2008
    241'.4—dc22

                                        2008019050

Printed in the United States of America
2008—First Edition

10 9 8 7 6 5 4 3 2 1

SPECIAL SALES
Most WaterBrook Multnomah books are available in special quantity discounts when purchased in bulk by corporations, organizations, and special-interest groups. Custom imprinting or excerpting can also be done to fit special needs. For information, please e-mail SpecialMarkets@WaterBrook Multnomah.com or call 1-800-603-7051.

Dedicated to Shelley Chapman McGuirt, M.D.

Acknowledgments

I am deeply indebted to my family of origin: Sam, Grace, and Sandra. My dad, mom, and sister gave me my first taste of love. Only Mom remains. At age ninety-seven she tells me, "I won't be here much longer and that's all right." Having spent my life working with dysfunctional families, I am aware of how fortunate I am to have been reared in a loving family.

I also have learned much about love from my wife, Karolyn, who for more than forty years has been my chief encourager. Daughter Shelley and son Derek have been loved from birth and now reciprocate love to us and to everyone they encounter. This book is dedicated to Shelley. She embodies love as well as anyone I have ever known. I am grateful to be her father.

I have enjoyed working with Elisa Stanford on this project. She has scouted out many of the stories that appear on these pages. Her diligence has kept us on track to complete the book in a timely fashion. Senior editor Ron Lee and production editor Pamela Shoup of the WaterBrook Multnomah Publishing Group have also been of immense help. It has been a pleasure to work with them.

Contents

Part 3: PATIENCE

Part 4: FORGIVENESS

Part 5: COURTESY

Part 6: HUMILITY

Part 9: MAKING LOVE A WAY OF LIFE EVERY DAY

Introduction

Christ longs for his followers to love as he loves. "A new command I give you: Love one another. As I have loved you, so you must love one another" (John 13:34). Christ not only raises the standard of love, but he also offers himself as the model. When we love as Christ loved, we are showing others the love of God.

In the book *Love as a Way of Life*, I named the seven distinguishing characteristics of a loving person: kindness, patience, forgiveness, courtesy, humility, generosity, and honesty. I believe that when we reflect these traits in daily life with neighbors, family members, co-workers, and even strangers, we are reflecting the love of Christ.

While *Love as a Way of Life* is intended to challenge you to action, this devotional book is designed to speak to your heart so that you might know more of the love of God in your own life as you learn to love others more. This book is divided into short readings that follow the order of the character traits of a loving person in *Love as a Way of Life*, including as well three introductory readings and three concluding readings. In light of the variety of stories, verses, and suggestions, the two books complement each other.

All the devotional readings are intended for personal quiet times with God, whether that's first thing in the morning, last thing at night, or during a break in the middle of the day. My hope is that my words will be springboards for prayer in your life. With that in mind, after each devotional I include a brief prayer, thought, or idea related to strengthening your relationship with God and prompting a life of love.

God wants his followers to be channels of his love. May this small book draw you closer to God so that you might be "filled to the measure of all the fullness of God" (Ephesians 3:19) and discover the joy of seeing Christ's love flow from you to others every day.

Part 1

LOVE AS A NEW WAY OF LIFE

Bedtime Stories

I am convinced that neither death nor life,
neither angels nor demons, neither the present nor the future, nor any powers, neither
height nor depth, nor anything else in all
creation, will be able to separate us from the
love of God that is in Christ Jesus our Lord.
—ROMANS 8:38–39

When my grandchildren were toddlers, I read many
books to them about farms, the alphabet, and how
to have good manners. A more subtle theme among children's picture books is unconditional love. "Mama, do you
love me?" a child asks her mother. "How much do you love
me?" a bunny asks his father. With a variety of settings and
characters, countless books represent children asking, "What

if I ran away? What if I hurt you? What if I traveled to the moon or broke a vase or hit my sister? Would you still love me?"

"Yes," the parent says. "I will love you no matter what. I will always love you."

These cozy bedtime stories reflect a universal need that we never outgrow: the need to know that someone, somewhere, loves us without restraint or condition. What a gift we give each other when we communicate that kind of love every day. We might not say it with words. In fact, we might choose to love by *not* speaking but by being patient in the face of frustration, kind when someone is rude to us, or humble when it would be easier to talk about our accomplishments. But every time we are purposeful about making love a way of life, we are affirming what we each need to hear— and what God speaks to us every day: You are loved. No matter what. Forever and always.

THOUGHT

How would truly believing God loves you—no matter what—change your thoughts and actions in the next twenty-four hours?

Easy to Find

Trust steadily in God, hope unswervingly,
love extravagantly. And the best of the
three is love.
     —1 CORINTHIANS 13:13, MSG

M ary Jo is easy to find," seven-year-old Richard tells a
visitor to the shelter. "Look for someone kind and
someone who is always smiling. She prays a lot too. She might
be praying or singing or helping people."

It's no wonder people have so little trouble recognizing
Mary Jo Copeland. She is the no-nonsense homemaker who
is washing the worn feet of homeless people before providing
them with clean socks and new shoes. "Look after your feet,"
she tells those she helps. "They must carry you a long way in
this world and then all the way to the kingdom of God." She

is the woman who once faced deep depression yet now welcomes the needy with a smile of joy. "I reach out to people as they are, not as I want them to be," Mary Jo says.

The founder and director of Sharing and Caring Hands, a nonprofit organization that cares for disadvantaged people in Minneapolis, Copeland oversees a network of services that helps thousands of individuals and families find food, homes, and new starts in life. As she reminds her volunteers, "When someone is drowning, you do more than throw a life preserver. You get into the water."

Whether our primary mission is similar to Mary Jo Copeland's or centered within our home or workplace, every time we choose to love someone in an unloving world, we are making ourselves known as followers of Christ. We are choosing to stand out—not for what we accomplish but for our willingness to make sacrifices. Like Jesus, we are reflecting the joy that comes from being genuine lovers who thrive on being "easy to find."

Prayer

*Lord, for your sake I want people's main
impression of me to be that I love others well.*

The Power to Love

> I have been crucified with Christ and I no
> longer live, but Christ lives in me.
> —GALATIANS 2:20

Most of the world's religions are based on human effort. Some religions encourage meditation and the repetition of mantras designed to free the mind of selfish desires. Other religions emphasize giving alms or repeating prayers or making a pilgrimage. But as Christians, we know that we can never do good and love others in our own power. We are morally flawed, and left to our own devices, we will be inwardly focused. We will seek our own happiness and not what is best for those around us.

Knowing the reality of our weaknesses, we can find great freedom in realizing that the key to becoming a loving person lies not with us but with God. It is *God's* love that we seek to share, not a love manufactured on our own. It is God's Spirit who pours love into us and enables us to give to others (see Romans 5:5). And it is Christ's life, death, and resurrection that give us a new perspective on life. That radical perspective focuses not on self but on our Creator. We have more than enough love to offer others because behind everything that exists in the universe is a personal God who loves us and wants to express his love through us.

PRAYER

*Holy Spirit, I want to receive your love
and express that love to others.*

Part 2

KINDNESS

Instruments
of Peace

How beautiful on the mountains are the
feet of those who bring good news, who
proclaim peace, who bring good tidings,
who proclaim salvation, who say to
Zion, "Your God reigns!"
—ISAIAH 52:7

More than eight hundred years ago, Francis of Assisi
prayed, "Lord, make me an instrument of your
peace; where there is hatred, let me sow love; where there is
injury, pardon; where there is doubt, faith; where there is despair, hope; where there is darkness, light; where there is sadness, joy." Sometimes when we hear the latest tragic story of

violence in the world, the idea of being instruments of peace can seem overwhelming. But small acts of kindness remind us that in the face of fear, injury, and hatred, good does exist. Good exists in the hands of volunteers who help build houses after natural disasters, in the sacrifices of military personnel fighting for someone else's safety, and in the simple ways we choose to serve others at work, at home, and in the community.

As Francis concluded, "It is in giving that we receive, it is in pardoning that we are pardoned, and it is in dying that we are born to eternal life." Acting kindly means dying to our selfish desires so that the needs of others might be met. Self-denial goes against everything the evening news suggests about human nature. But when we live out God's kindness in ordinary ways, even moments of despair can become opportunities for hope.

PRAYER

*In a violent world, Father, remind me
of the peace I can offer others through
practicing simple kindness.*

Special Delivery

Dear friends, let us love one another, for
love comes from God.
                    —1 JOHN 4:7

It was two days before Christmas. I was helping my wife
take care of holiday details when I noticed a van parked
in front of our house. I watched as the driver got out—it was
my friend Joe Warner. As Joe proceeded to the back of his
van, I knew what was about to happen, because it has happened every Christmas for the last several years. He pulled
out a box filled with the best, sweetest oranges and walked
toward our house. His halting gait reminded me of the injury
he suffered in World War II.

I opened the front door before Joe rang the bell, and I
welcomed him inside. "Merry Christmas!" he said as he set

the box of oranges on the floor. After I thanked him for remembering us with this kindness, I asked about his family and he asked about mine. We said our good-byes and he was gone.

As I watched Joe walk back to the van, I experienced a strong sense of gratitude for a friend who, in his eighties, continues to do such acts of kindness. Joe's kindness was not a matter of responding to human need—he knew I could buy my own oranges. It was pure love shown in a small but significant way.

I believe God delights in such gentle kindnesses. And every Christmas, Joe Warner gives me a new opportunity to catch a glimpse of Christ's love in a box of oranges.

PRAYER

Father, thank you for the people in my life
who show me kindness in simple ways.

The Attitude
of Christ

When [Jesus] saw the crowds, he had
compassion on them, because they were
harassed and helpless, like sheep without
a shepherd.

—MATTHEW 9:36

A young businessman named Michael told me that he never realized how unkind he could be until he asked God to show him. "Each night for a week I prayed for God to make me aware of ways I was being unkind. That was a prayer that he answered. It didn't take long for me to see how I needed to change my words and actions.

"Recently I tried to help a colleague who was going

through a crisis. In the middle of our conversation, he said, 'I think I might need to go to church with you. I think I need some spiritual help.' I don't remember ever discussing spiritual things with him, but I had tried to treat him with kindness. After he went to church with me, we talked about the life of Jesus and his purposes for us. Within three months, he became a transformed Christian. He had responded to God's love, and his life was in the process of changing."

Michael learned how to see people as individuals, created in the image of God, each gifted by God to play a particular role in life, and capable of having a love relationship with God. He had developed the attitude of Christ.

As Michael realized, the world is filled with people who are like sheep without a shepherd. We are called to share the love of God—and as we do, we see how powerful kindness can be.

ACTION STEP

At the end of each day for the next week, ask God to show you ways you were unkind that day. Make a commitment to show kindness no matter how frustrating things get during the day. And if you realize you have hurt someone, apologize to that person.

God's Embrace

I led them with cords of human kindness,
with ties of love; I lifted the yoke from
their neck and bent down to feed them.
—HOSEA 11:4

Child psychologists tell us that when a child is secure in her parents' love, she is more eager to interact with others and develop her own relationships. She knows that she can always return to the loving embrace of her mother or father.

God longs for us to trust his love the way a child trusts the love of a parent. Kindness is a part of God's love—demonstrated in his tender care. In fact, God's kindness is often translated as "steadfast love" in the Hebrew Bible. No matter the circumstances, difficulties, or fears of life, God's loving-kindness is constant. Because of the security we have in that love, we are free to be kind to others. We care for others from the center of God's care for us.

The beautiful reality is that God gives us many opportunities to be kind, and he gives us great joy when we are kind. The pleasure we know in caring for others is just a shadow of the delight he takes in caring for us.

THOUGHT

When has God's kindness motivated
you to be kind to someone else?

Strong Words

It is I, speaking in righteousness, mighty
to save.

—ISAIAH 63:1

The religious leaders thought they had finally trapped
Jesus. Perhaps smugly, they brought out a woman who
had been caught in adultery. They exposed her sin publicly,
knowing their law required the death penalty for such a
woman. Yet Jesus said, "If any one of you is without sin, let
him be the first to throw a stone at her." At that, the leaders
began to walk away, and only Jesus was left with the woman.
He said to her, "Woman, where are they? Has no one con-
demned you?"

"No one, sir," she answered.

"Then neither do I condemn you," Jesus said. "Go now and leave your life of sin" (John 8:7–11).

Jesus had every right to wield his power and boast of his perfection that day. Yet consider the kindness in his words. He helped the accusers gain a bigger perspective: Every one of us is a sinner. It is not our place to judge another person. God is the Judge. Then Jesus spoke words of kindness to the woman. He did not condone her sin, but he offered her a chance to choose a better life. Jesus's words were quietly powerful because of the love behind them.

We can learn a lot from Jesus's example. If we wait until the people around us rise to a higher standard before we speak words of kindness, we may never speak. But if we take every opportunity to show the power of kind words, God can work through us to change lives.

THOUGHT

When you are tempted to think kindness
shows weakness, remember that God shows
his power through kind words.

Created for Kindness

In the image of God he created him;
male and female he created them.
—GENESIS 1:27

Arecent study at the Yale University Infant Cognition Center reminds us that we are created to show and receive kindness. In the study, researchers had babies—ranging in age from six to ten months—watch a wooden toy try to climb to the top of a roller-coaster incline. As the toy climbed, some toys came along to help it over the top, while others came along to push it back down. Then the babies were given the chance to play with any of the toys. Almost every child chose the toys that had helped!

We are created in the image of a kind God. That means we are drawn to kindness—and even search for it—from the time we are very young. We never lose our need for kindness, but as adults we sometimes value ambition and prestige more. Particularly in the business world, it can be easy to forget that our minds and emotions were made to respond to kindness, not harshness.

When we act kindly toward others, they will be drawn to us and to God. That's why being kind is so energizing. When we are kind, we are acting as we were created to act.

PRAYER

*Dear God, I want to choose every day to act
and speak in the way you created me to.*

Standing Out

As God's chosen people, holy and dearly
loved, clothe yourselves with compassion, kindness, humility, gentleness and
patience.
—COLOSSIANS 3:12

In the later centuries of the Roman Empire—and the early
centuries of the Christian era—the once-proud empire
suffered a series of setbacks. Wars, waves of invasion by Ger-
manic tribes, and devastating epidemics led to a fractured,
failing society.

In the face of terrible conditions, political elites and their
non-Christian priests fled the cities. The only functioning
social network left was the church, which provided basic nurs-
ing care to Christians and non-Christians alike, along with

hope that transcended death. Even pagans acknowledged that early Christians were as kind to their neighbors as they would be to family. What made the church so powerful during that time was not artful persuasion but serving others with love.

The world is much different today, of course, but we have similar opportunities to show kindness to others. Think about the Asian tsunami of 2004 and Hurricane Katrina in the United States in 2005. Our nation responded to both catastrophes. But in many instances the church was the vehicle through which help continued to arrive. Christ-followers wanted to make a difference in others' lives, simply for the sake of sharing love. The influence of such acts of kindness is immeasurable. As history shows, entire cultures can change as a result of the Christian community practicing the love of Christ.

PRAYER

*Thank you, Lord, for using things as simple
as acts of kindness to point people to you.*

Eyes of Love

Jesus looked at him and loved him.
—MARK 10:21

Benny was eleven years old the first time he went with his mom to cook a meal at a homeless shelter. He arrived there expecting to see dirty, cranky, hungry people, but he found something entirely different. That evening he met "regular guys" with families, hopes, and abilities.

"They were nice," Benny said. "We talked to them.… A lot of them had jobs; they just didn't have enough money to get a place to stay."

Something happens when we love other people: we begin to see them as God sees them. We might first choose to be kind out of obedience, but we continue to be kind because our love for others grows as we live out the love of Jesus.

Obedience fills us with joy, not a sense of obligation. We see others' strengths, hopes, and needs. We become aware of their goodness when we share goodness with them—even as we realize that we share many of their dreams and fears. Kindness gives us the opportunity to recognize beautiful people who are in need of Christ. Just like us.

PRAYER

God, I want to see through your eyes
when I look at other people.

Out of Control

Your attitude should be the same as that of
Christ Jesus: Who…made himself noth-
ing, taking the very nature of a servant.
—PHILIPPIANS 2:5–7

What is most likely to prevent you from showing love
to someone else? Many of us try to protect ourselves from being hurt or taken advantage of. And sometimes
we wonder if the other person really *deserves* our kindness.

In *Letters to an American Lady,* C. S. Lewis wrote, "It will
not bother me in the hour of death to reflect that I have been
'had for a sucker' by any number of imposters; but it would
be a torment to know that one had refused even one person
in need." To be kind is to be vulnerable. Every act of kindness is a way of saying, *I want to care for you no matter how*

you respond. I will put myself in a weaker position so that I can help you.

The life of Christ reminds us that only when we take the attitude of a servant can we grow into the character of God. Every time we serve someone else, the results are out of our control—who knows how the other person will react? Yet those are the moments when we understand Christ's love for us most deeply. Those are the moments when we know what *true* strength is.

PRAYER

Dear Father, help me to see opportunities for servanthood as opportunities to know you more.

Do the Impossible

Since we live by the Spirit, let us keep in
step with the Spirit.
                    —GALATIANS 5:25

Caring for my teenage stepson since he's been living with
us is one of the hardest things I've had to do," Krista
told me. "The turning point for me came when I stopped
worrying about how I would handle all the future days and
started asking for God's Spirit to work through me *that* day.
Then what seemed impossible became reality. I still strug-
gled, but I was amazed at how God helped me to be kind
when the selfish part of me wanted to run out the door."

The Spirit of God is available to help us do what might
seem impossible: love our co-workers, family members, and
strangers with the love of Christ. God empowers us to develop

the character traits of Christ. He gives us his Spirit so that he can love others through us. So why do we waste so much effort trying to *feel* loving?

If the call to be kind seems difficult to you right now, take heart. God is in you to reflect his love in ways you never could on your own.

ACTION STEP

*Think about one person you will encounter
this week who seems impossible to love.
Ask the Holy Spirit to show God's kindness
to that person through you.*

Dream Builder

> Now to him who is able to do immeasurably more than all we ask or imagine, according to his power that is at work within us, to him be glory.
> —EPHESIANS 3:20–21

Jenna Glatzer grew up in a poor neighborhood without the luxuries many children enjoy. Even though her father did not have much money, as Glatzer recalls, he "was a man on a mission to make me feel like a princess." Her father even used hand-me-down tools and donated materials to build Jenna a Cinderella castle in their backyard. Years later Jenna wrote, "My treasures weren't stored in the walls of the castle. They were stored in memories…. That's the legacy of a father's love that no swing set can ever replace."

God uses us to care for one another's practical needs and also for the needs of each other's souls—including the soul of a child with princess dreams. In doing so, the Lord reminds us that he is aware of our deep longings as well as the daily realities of our lives. When we ask God to reveal the hearts of those around us, we become aware of how we might be a part of helping God build his dreams in someone else's life.

PRAYER

*Jesus, help me be aware of how
others need to be loved.*

Unending Kindness

I will betroth you…in love and compassion.
—HOSEA 2:19

How many of us love with *unending* kindness—especially when our love is not returned? The challenge to love others in the face of rejection is not new. In biblical times, God told his story of kindness to a wayward Israel through the prophet Hosea. Hosea's wife, Gomer, was repeatedly unfaithful. "I will go after my lovers, who give me my food and my water, my wool and my linen, my oil and my drink" (Hosea 2:5). Yet Hosea took Gomer back again and again, promising, "I will betroth you to me forever; I will betroth you in righteousness and justice, in love and compassion" (verse 2:19).

God used Hosea to remind Israel—and us—that his

kindness does not end when we turn away from him. He longs for us to come back.

Has God called you to show kindness to someone who rarely responds with kindness? Do you love someone who rejects your love? Perhaps, like Hosea, you are a spouse who has been betrayed. In the midst of your pain, believe that God understands what it is like to have kindness rejected. He comes alongside you to love others when it is most difficult. The desire to be kind to those who fail to respond with kindness is one of the miracles of following Christ. It reminds us of a God who, even in hurt and anger, allows kindness to prevail.

PRAYER

Lord, thank you for loving me so much
that you never stop pursuing me.

Part 3

PATIENCE

Lifelong Prayers

Imitate those who through faith and
patience inherit what has been promised.
—HEBREWS 6:12

Augustine of Hippo (AD 354–430) was one of the most important thinkers and leaders in early church history. His influence on Western Christianity is still felt today. What many do not know is that Augustine's conversion to Christ came after thirty-two years of his mother's patient and faithful prayer.

Augustine's devout mother, Monica, watched her son reject the Bible, move in with his girlfriend and have a child by her, get involved in a religious sect, leave his girlfriend and become engaged to a young heiress, and break the engagement and move on to other lovers, all the while pursuing his education. Every time Augustine moved to a different city to attend another school, his mother moved to that city and continued praying.

In 386, at the age of thirty-two, Augustine had an encounter with Christ that changed his life. He resigned his teaching post in Milan and returned with his son to Thagaste, his hometown in North Africa, to follow Christ. Monica lived long enough to see the answer to her prayers.

Through her unchanging love and commitment, Monica emulated the patience of God. God allows his children to grow and develop as they move toward Christlikeness. Even when we fail, he never gives up on us.

PRAYER

Father, when my own failures discourage me,
help me remember that you are still
patiently at work in my life.

The Patience of God

You, O Lord, are a compassionate and
gracious God, slow to anger, abounding
in love and faithfulness.
            —PSALM 86:15

We sometimes think of the God of the Old Testament
as a God of anger who was constantly bringing
judgment on people. In truth, the God revealed in *both* the
Old and New Testaments has two distinct characteristics: justice and love.

God's justice is often described by the Hebrew word for
holy. The word literally means "set apart." God alone is set
apart to execute justice. But the second essential characteristic

of God's nature is love, and one way he expresses his love is through patience.

The Hebrew word for "patient" is *arek*, meaning "long," as in "long (or slow) to anger." Jeremiah the prophet described God as "long-suffering," or patient (Jeremiah 15:15). And through Isaiah, God said to his rebellious people, "For my own name's sake I delay my wrath; for the sake of my praise I hold it back from you, so as not to cut you off" (Isaiah 48:9).

When we are patient with others, even in small ways, we are reflecting the character of a loving God.

THOUGHT

Mentally review the history of God's patience
with you. Thank him for his patient love.

Danger Ahead

"In your anger do not sin": Do not let
the sun go down while you are still angry,
and do not give the devil a foothold.
—EPHESIANS 4:26–27

A study of nine thousand British civil servants, reported in the *Archives of Internal Medicine,* found that prolonged anger is bad for one's health. Participants who were involved in hostile, critical relationships were 34 percent more likely to have a heart attack or chest pain compared to participants who had emotional support and frequent opportunities to voice their feelings in a healthy way.

Anger in itself is not necessarily wrong. But impatient anger that fails to take the other person's needs into account can be destructive. That's one of the reasons why it's so important to show patience in our words and actions, even when we are upset with someone. Patience gives us a chance to apply reason to the emotions that might otherwise cause us to do or say something unloving.

Ephesians 4:26–27 reminds us that controlling our anger is a spiritual issue. When we fail to control our anger, we give Satan an opportunity to attack us—and our minds, bodies, and relationships all take a beating.

ACTION STEP

Picture a situation you sometimes find yourself in that triggers anger. Now, commit yourself to take a step—such as counting to ten, leaving the room, or putting your hand over your mouth—that will help you use patience to control your anger.

The Beauty Remains

Be joyful in hope, patient in affliction,
faithful in prayer.
—ROMANS 12:12

The French artist Pierre Auguste Renoir was a leader in the early Impressionist movement of the nineteenth century. For the last two decades of his life, Renoir had to adapt his painting style to accommodate debilitating rheumatoid arthritis. He sometimes strapped a brush to his immobile, deformed fingers in order to continue his work. He also took up sculpting, directing others to act as his hands. He completed some of his most famous works when he was in the advanced stages of his illness.

One of Renoir's closest friends was the artist Henri Matisse. On one occasion, as Matisse watched his friend struggle to apply each brushstroke, Matisse asked, "Why do you continue to paint when you are in such agony?"

Renoir replied, "The beauty remains; the pain passes."

Renoir's words remind us of the hope God offers when we are patient in the face of disappointment and pain. One of the two Greek words translated as "patience" in the New Testament is *hypomone,* which means "to remain under." This kind of patience speaks of being faithful to God's calling even when things seem hopeless, and loving others even when they seem unlovable. It speaks of trusting that our pain will pass but the beauty of God's work in us—and through us—will remain for eternity.

PRAYER

*Father, help me to live with a
focus on what will last.*

Patience Means Salvation

> The Lord is not slow in keeping his promise, as some understand slowness. He is patient with you, not wanting anyone to perish, but everyone to come to repentance.
>
> —2 PETER 3:9

L
ike all the traits of love, patience is more than just "a nice way to act." When we are patient, we are reflecting God's patience—a patience that leads not to warm, fuzzy feelings but to spiritual transformation. As the apostle Peter said, "Our Lord's patience means salvation" (2 Peter 3:15).

It's hard to believe that God might use our small act of

patience to show someone his love—or even bring someone to faith in God—but he does. After all, it is God's patience with us that leads *us* to salvation. Had he chosen to show immediate justice for the wrongs we've committed, none of us would be alive. Because of his loving patience, God allowed us to go on with life so that we might discover that he desires to have a relationship with us. God's patience toward us spurs us to be patient with others so that they might receive the mercy we know.

ACTION STEP

Whenever you start to think your actions don't make a big difference, recall the phrase "patience means salvation" (2 Peter 3:15).

Under Construction

He who began a good work in you will
carry it on to completion until the day
of Christ Jesus.

—PHILIPPIANS 1:6

When Ruth Bell Graham died in 2007, she left
behind a legacy of love and servanthood. At her
funeral in Montreat, North Carolina, thousands gathered to
remember this writer, poet, mother, and wife, who stood by
the side of her husband, evangelist Billy Graham, for nearly
sixty-four years.

One of Ruth's striking characteristics was her awareness
of God's continual work in her—an awareness that freed her

to be patient with herself and others. Ruth once saw a message on a highway sign that she wanted on her gravestone: "End of construction. Thank you for your patience."

When we are aware that *we* are still growing, changing, and becoming more like Christ, we will be much more patient with others who are also in process. When we forget that we ourselves are not as we would like to be, we are more likely to become impatient with others. How freeing it is to remember that each of us is still under God's construction! We love others with patience, knowing that one day they will be complete just as we will be.

PRAYER

Lord, thank you for giving me a good
reason to be patient with others:
the fact that, like them, I'm not yet perfect.

Paying Off a Debt

When you, a mere man, pass judgment on
them and yet do the same things, do you
think you will escape God's judgment? Or do
you show contempt for the riches of his kindness, tolerance and patience, not realizing that
God's kindness leads you toward repentance?
—ROMANS 2:3–4

Jesus told the story of a king who wanted "to settle accounts with his servants." One man owed him ten thousand talents (a vast sum). When called to sell his wife, children, and all his possessions to pay off the debt, the man pleaded with the king. " 'Be patient with me,…and I will pay back everything.' The servant's master took pity on him, canceled the debt and let him go."

Some time later this same servant demanded the repayment of a debt of one hundred denarii (a relatively small amount) owed him by a fellow servant. "His fellow servant fell to his knees and begged him, 'Be patient with me, and I will pay you back.' But he refused. Instead, he went off and had the man thrown into prison until he could pay the debt." The king found the servant who was unwilling to be patient with his debtor and put him in prison, saying, "Shouldn't you have had mercy on your fellow servant just as I had on you?" (Matthew 18:23, 26–30, 33).

This is one of the most powerful examples we have of why we need to be patient with others. Their obligations might be financial, as in this story, or relational, as we wait for someone to respond to our love. God shows patience with us even when we can't pay him back for all his gifts. We are to reflect his love by showing the same patience to others.

ACTION STEP

Today, whenever you are tempted to be impatient with someone, remember a recent time when God or a person was patient with you.

Be Still

Be still, and know that I am God.
—PSALM 46:10

Having a quiet, patient spirit throughout the day is countercultural in our harried world, but its effects can be life changing for us as well as for others. People notice when we are patient with strangers in line, with our kids at the park, and with our co-workers in meetings, because it is so much more common to show impatience. A patient stillness in attitude, words, and behavior, even in the midst of stress, always stands out.

Author Eugene Peterson reminds us how this kind of radical patience allows room for us to grow closer to others: "When we are noisy and when we are hurried, we are incapable of intimacy—deep, complex, personal relationships."

While an anxious spirit on our part makes others feel more rushed and frustrated, a quiet spirit is likely to calm those around us, making loving interactions more possible. So not only does a patient spirit still the noise of the world so we can enjoy deeper peace, it also helps to still the noise in others' lives so we can enjoy one another more fully.

ACTION STEP

When you feel yourself getting anxious or rushed during the day, remember the words "Be still," and focus on having a peaceful spirit instead of a harried one.

Decades of Prayer

Wait for the LORD; be strong and take
heart and wait for the LORD.
—PSALM 27:14

In 1951, Don Fields stole a Gideon Bible from a hotel room, took it back to his naval base, and started reading it. Three months later, Don cried out to God that he needed help. As Don writes, "That is the point when I believed."

Don prayed regularly for his parents and two brothers. But it wasn't until seven years later, when Don's father was on a drinking binge, that Don's mom made a commitment to God. Soon Don began to spend more time with his dad, opening doors to conversation. One night a number of years later, his dad, in a drunken daze, called Don and said he wanted to become a Christian. Don knew his dad was drunk and questioned his words. But after his dad sobered up, he invited Don over to talk, and three weeks later he became a Christian. That was twenty-two years after Don's conversion.

Twelve years later, Don's brother Bob was diagnosed with cancer. The brothers started studying the Bible together by mail, and Bob accepted Christ a few months before he died. When Don's brother Philip was diagnosed with a brain tumor a year and a half later, he resisted God. Then on a trip to visit relatives, the two brothers started talking about spiritual things. The next year Philip became a believer.

"For thirty-eight years I prayed for my family," Don says. "Much of that time I would not have felt that there was much chance that they would become Christians, but I prayed for them and continued to talk to them about God. God is faithful and sure in doing his work in his own time." Patience calls us to remember that God loves those closest to us even more than we do.

PRAYER

God, I know that as I struggle to be patient,
you love _____ even more than I do.

Waiting for God's Calling

Let us fix our eyes on Jesus, the author
and perfecter of our faith, who for the
joy set before him endured the cross,
scorning its shame, and sat down at the
right hand of the throne of God.

—Hebrews 12:2

Do you sometimes get anxious for life to "begin"? You think, *When this project is done, I'll…* Or *When the kids grow up, we'll…* Or *When I graduate, I'll be able to…*

There's nothing wrong with dreaming about the future, but sometimes we get so impatient for life to change that we miss what God is doing right now. For the first thirty years of his life, Jesus waited to begin his public ministry. At the age of twelve, Jesus could answer questions in the temple in a way that amazed the teachers of the Law (see Luke 2:47). Even so, he waited another eighteen years before he began teaching and performing miracles.

In fact, for most of his adult life, Jesus practiced carpentry. Perhaps he wondered why God waited so long to initiate his formal ministry. But God knew the perfect number of days Jesus needed to complete his work on earth. The years of waiting were also part of Jesus's calling.

In patiently following God's plan, Jesus set the example for us. Patiently waiting for God means *actively* waiting for God—being aware of what he is doing in our lives today, how he is preparing us for the future, and what he is calling us to learn.

PRAYER

Father, I want to trust you, but sometimes I'm not sure what it looks like to wait for you. Help me to understand the calling you have for me.

Higher Ways

"My thoughts are not your thoughts,
neither are your ways my ways," declares
the LORD.

—ISAIAH 55:8

I often meet Christians who are upset because God hasn't answered their prayers—at least not in the way they had hoped or on their time schedule. Being patient with God does not mean believing that *he* is still in process but believing that he knows—better than we do—that *we* are still in process. Being patient with God means trusting that he is sovereign and loving. It means believing that his love will not allow him to answer requests that don't line up with his ultimate purposes.

We are not the first to grow restless when God's timing

appears to be off. Thousands of years ago, God reminded the prophet Isaiah, "As the heavens are higher than the earth, so are my ways higher than your ways and my thoughts than your thoughts" (Isaiah 55:9).

When we know that God is loving and just, we don't have to understand his ways in order to be at peace in the midst of life's stresses. We can accept that God operates on his own timetable. As the British hymn writer Frederick William Faber wrote, "We must wait for God, long, meekly, in the wind and wet, in the thunder and lightning, in the cold and the dark. Wait, and he will come. He never comes to those who do not wait."

PRAYER

Dear Lord, help me to trust that you love me
even when I don't understand your timing.

Accepting the Journey

What a gift life is to those who stay the
course! You've heard, of course, of Job's
staying power, and you know how God
brought it all together for him at the end.
That's because God cares, cares right
down to the last detail.
　　　　—JAMES 5:10–11, MSG

When my father died, my sister Sandra and her husband, Reid, bought the house next door to theirs
and made a home for my mother. The plan was that, as
Mother got older, Sandra would take care of her. In the prov-
idence of God, however, my mother ended up taking care of

my sister. At the age of fifty-three, my sister discovered she had cancer. With each passing year her condition worsened, and at fifty-eight she went home to be with Christ.

During those five years, I watched Sandra face adversity with patience. In the early stages, she drove herself to treatments and took my mother along for companionship. As her condition worsened, she accepted help from her husband and friends who volunteered to drive her to appointments. As long as she was able, she baby-sat her grandson. When Sandra's energy level would no longer permit baby-sitting, she let go of that grandmotherly pleasure.

Sandra wanted to live, yet never once did I hear her complain. She patiently accepted the journey that was laid out before her, demonstrating her confidence that whether she lived or died, her life was pointing people toward Christ.

I can only pray that when the time comes, I will demonstrate the same level of patience that I saw in Sandra's life. I believe such patience is a gift of God, given to those who are willing to accept it.

PRAYER

Father, I want my life to show a quiet patience that points people to you.

Part 4

FORGIVENESS

"All I Have to Offer"

Mercy triumphs over judgment!
—JAMES 2:13

Immaculée Ilibagiza was in her early twenties when tribal tensions exploded in her home country of Rwanda. Nearly a million Rwandans were killed during one hundred days of horror. Ilibagiza survived by hiding in a tiny bathroom with eight other women. When the killing finally ceased, she had lost nearly all her family.

Ilibagiza later had the opportunity to meet Felicien, the leader of the gang that killed her mother and brother. Felicien looked at Ilibagiza and met her eyes with shame. Then the young woman said what she had come to say: "I forgive you."

As Ilibagiza writes, "My heart eased immediately, and I saw the tension release in Felicien's shoulders." The guards led him back to his cell.

The man who had arrested Felicien asked Ilibagiza how she could respond that way. Ilibagiza answered, "Forgiveness is all I have to offer."

Ilibagiza's words reflect the Christlike choice to forgive. It was a *choice* because she had to let her desire for love win out over her desire for justice. Felicien never verbalized a response to Ilibagiza's offer of forgiveness, but Ilibagiza's spirit was free of anger. She left her concern for justice in the hands of God and government. She refused to seek revenge.

Today, Immaculée Ilibagiza travels around the world with her message of forgiveness. She has cared for Rwandan children orphaned in the genocide and worked with the United Nations to bring healing to her country. Only Christ's love can take energy that might be spent in anger and turn it into energy spent in love.

PRAYER

Lord, I want to enjoy the freedom
of forgiving others.

Change of Heart

Above all, love each other deeply, because
love covers over a multitude of sins.

—1 PETER 4:8

The first time I cheated on a test, it was easy," Marilyn
recalls. "The cheating itself, that is. But after I walked
out of the classroom, I felt terrible. All I could think was, *I've
disappointed my favorite teacher.* Then the test grades came
out, and it felt great to be at the head of the class. So I did it
again. And again.

"Somewhere near the end of that semester, the guilt got
to be too much. I went over to Mrs. Marlow's desk, and before I could say anything, I burst into tears. She put her arms
around me. I kept saying, 'You don't understand,' because of
course she wouldn't be comforting me if she knew what I'd

done. I told her everything. The worst part was the look of sadness on her face as she listened.

"When I finished talking, she looked me in the eyes and said, 'Marilyn, I forgive you. I'm glad you were able to tell me.'

"I received a C in physics that semester, after working hard with Mrs. Marlow after school and retaking the exams. Even with all that studying, I don't remember much about physics. I do remember how much Mrs. Marlow's forgiveness meant to me. When I became a Christian years later, I looked back at that moment as an important step toward realizing the forgiveness of Christ. Mrs. Marlow never knew what a difference her love made in my life. But she helped me see just how powerful words of forgiveness can be."

THOUGHT

*When has someone offering you
their forgiveness made a difference
in your life later on?*

Love Alone

Blessed is he whose transgressions
are forgiven, whose sins are covered.
Blessed is the man whose sin the
LORD does not count against him
and in whose spirit is no deceit.
—PSALM 32:1–2

When David, the second king of Israel, committed adultery with Bathsheba and then plotted the death of Bathsheba's husband, God loved him too much to let him live with his sin. Here is how David described God's conviction: "When I kept silent, my bones wasted away through my groaning all day long. For day and night your hand was heavy upon me" (Psalm 32:3–4). God knew that only when David confessed his sin could he live out his calling.

When we follow God's example, love alone prompts us to confront someone who has done wrong, receive his apology, and grant pardon. We forgive because we want our offender to be free. We celebrate with him when he confesses, because we know God celebrates with us when we confess.

That's why the first step in becoming a loving person is to acknowledge our own sinful behavior. That helps us avoid turning an opportunity to forgive into a moment of superiority. We cannot give what we have not received. When we have experienced the love that leads God to pardon our sins, we are able to extend that love to others.

PRAYER

Father, sometimes I forget that you convict
me of sin because you love me. Thank you
for wanting me to be more like you.

Am I Worth It?

What I have forgiven—if there was anything to forgive—I have forgiven in the
sight of Christ for your sake.

—2 CORINTHIANS 2:10

In Fyodor Dostoevsky's classic *The Brothers Karamazov,* the priest Zosima tells the story of the life he lived before committing himself to God. The turning point came in the days after he learned that the woman he loved had married another man. At one point Zosima was in such "a savage and brutal humor" over losing her that he beat his orderly, Afanasy, until the man's face was covered in blood.

The next morning, Zosima felt in his heart something "vile and shameful." As he describes later, "That is what a man has been brought to, and that was a man beating a fellow creature! What a crime!"

Zosima ran into Afanasy's room and asked for forgiveness. When he saw that Afanasy looked frightened, Zosima, in his officer's uniform, bowed his head to the ground in front of his servant and said again, "Forgive me."

Afanasy was stunned. "Your honor...sir, what are you doing? Am I worth it?"

Although he was Afanasy's master, in begging forgiveness, Zosima was saying, *We are equals. I value you. You are worthy of my asking for your pardon.* Asking for forgiveness affirms the value of another person. When someone comes to us to apologize for something, she is saying, *You are worth it to me. This relationship is worth it to me.* Our best response is to receive that affirmation and forgive.

PRAYER

*Father, when people apologize to me,
help me recognize what they are trying
to say and offer genuine forgiveness.*

Amen!

Be kind and compassionate to one
another, forgiving each other, just as
in Christ God forgave you.
—EPHESIANS 4:32

How do we cooperate with God and become more forgiving people? We first must say amen to God's purposes.

Amen is a Hebrew word that means "I agree" or "Let it be so." When we read or hear about our calling to forgive others, our response should be, "Amen—I agree, let it be so." Then we remain open to letting God teach us to show mercy and grace.

Christianity is about having a love relationship with God. In that relationship, he allows us to cooperate with him in what he is doing in the world. God wants to use us to express his love to others so that they, too, may have the opportunity of receiving and reciprocating his love.

As Paul reminds us in Ephesians, kindness, compassion, and forgiveness intersect. When we choose to forgive others instead of looking at their faults, it's not about our trying to "feel" forgiving, but about God using us to express his forgiveness. Our part is to agree with him!

PRAYER

Dear Lord, I want my life to be
characterized by grace. Let it be so!

Apology Accepted

Do not judge, and you will not be judged.
Do not condemn, and you will not be con-
demned. Forgive, and you will be forgiven.
—LUKE 6:37

When I met Karolyn, I knew I had found the woman who would satisfy my longing for intimacy. Of course, I intended to make her happy as well. Six months after we got married, however, we were both miserable. I found myself saying harsh, cutting words to the one I loved. And she reciprocated.

I let resentment build up toward Karolyn. I knew that I should apologize, but so should she, I reasoned. So I waited, but no apology came, and we grew further apart.

When eventually I turned to God for help, his message

was clear: "You need to take responsibility and apologize to your wife." I knew that my first step was to acknowledge my failure to God. I told him what a horrible job I had done as a husband, and I asked for his forgiveness.

That evening I apologized to Karolyn, naming as many of my failures as I could remember. "If you will forgive me," I said, "I want to make the future different." She hugged me and admitted her failures, and we forgave each other.

Good marriages do not require perfection, but they do require confession and forgiveness. Forgiveness releases the wrongs of the past and opens the door to the possibility of a better future.

PRAYER

God, give me the strength to apologize in my closest relationships, whether or not the other person apologizes to me.

Radiant Joy

Her many sins have been forgiven—for
she loved much. But he who has been
forgiven little loves little.
—LUKE 7:47

On February 3, 1998, Karla Faye Tucker was executed
for murdering two people during an attempted robbery. Her story made national news, not only because she
would be the first woman executed in Texas since the Civil
War, but also because she had become a Christian while in
prison.

Tucker spoke freely about the source of her joy: the forgiveness of God. Early in her prison sentence she had "stolen"
a Bible from a prison-ministry group, not knowing it was

free. She began reading, then crying, then asking God to forgive her.

"That's when the whole weight of what I did fell on me," she described later. "I realized for the first time that I had brutally murdered two people and there were people out there hurting because of me. Yet God was saying, 'I love you.'"

Tucker lived out a Christ-given peace, bringing many of her fellow prisoners to a deeper understanding of their need for forgiveness. Her story is a beautiful reminder to those who fear that forgiveness is a passive response to wrongdoing. True forgiveness does not gloss over sin but shows us how sinful we are—and how good God is. True forgiveness leaves no one unchanged.

PRAYER

Father, I acknowledge your love for me and ask
forgiveness for_____ today.

This I Know

This…is how we know that we belong to
the truth, and how we set our hearts at
rest in his presence whenever our hearts
condemn us. For God is greater than our
hearts, and he knows everything.
—1 JOHN 3:19–20

When Mao Zedong came to power in China in 1949, the Chinese church suffered great persecution. Friends in other parts of the world rarely heard news from Chinese Christians. Then in 1972 a message came to the United States with this explanation: "The 'This I Know' people are well." The authorities let the letter pass, not knowing it referred to one of the most beloved hymns of the faith, "Jesus Loves Me."

Anna Warner's hymn, written in 1859, has comforted millions over the years with its simple declaration: "Jesus loves me, this I know." Perhaps this is the most important thing for us to remember when we struggle to accept God's forgiveness. Sometimes, after we acknowledge our sin, Satan continues to accuse us. *You're just going to do it again. Don't you think God gets tired of forgiving you?* he taunts. That's when we respond with what we know to be true: *Jesus loves me. Jesus died for that sin. This I know.* The more we return to that fundamental truth, the more God's forgiveness frees us to reach out to others with forgiveness.

Every time we receive God's forgiveness or extend forgiveness to someone else, we are declaring again that no matter what Satan says, we are "this I know" people.

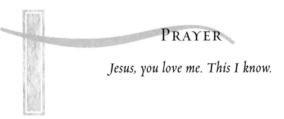

PRAYER

Jesus, you love me. This I know.

The Best Judge

Do not take revenge, my friends, but
leave room for God's wrath, for it is
written: "It is mine to avenge; I will
repay," says the Lord.
—ROMANS 12:19

Desert fathers from the fourth century said, "Judging
others is a heavy burden." When someone refuses to
apologize to us, the biblical challenge is to *release* the person to
God, along with our hurt and anger. If the offender confesses
and repents, God will forgive her and so can we. If she does
not repent, God will bring judgment. When you release someone to God, you are putting that person in good hands. When
you release your hurt and anger to God, you are relinquishing

to God your right to execute justice—and freeing yourself of a great burden.

Jesus set the standard. The apostle Peter said of Christ, "When they hurled insults at him, he did not retaliate; when he suffered, he made no threats. Instead, he entrusted himself to him who judges justly" (1 Peter 2:23). Jesus refused to take revenge on those who had wronged him. Instead, he committed the situation to his Father, knowing that God would judge righteously.

When we are wronged, it's tempting to think that if we don't demand justice, no one will. But God is in a far better position to be the Judge. We can turn the offender and the wrong that was committed over to God, knowing that he will take the best possible action on our behalf.

PRAYER

Lord, forgive me for wanting to judge someone instead of letting you be the Judge.

Letting Go
of the Past

He forgave us all our sins, having canceled
the written code, with its regulations, that
was against us and that stood opposed to
us; he took it away, nailing it to the cross.
—COLOSSIANS 2:13–14

On December 28, 2007, dozens of New Yorkers decided to leave the past in the past. A business group and the city's sanitation department issued an invitation to bring hurts and grudges to Times Square, where recycling bins and a five-foot-tall industrial shredder were ready to dispose of bad memories. Organizers also provided stationery so passersby could write down and then shred the pain they wanted to let go of.

People came to rid themselves of everything from drug addiction to disappointing report cards to old letters, bad loans, and abusive bosses. Many people said they were letting go of anger they had held toward a person who betrayed them. An hour after the shredder was set up, a sanitation truck carted away the debris, leaving many New Yorkers with smiles of relief.

Getting rid of relational wounds through a symbolic act can be a good way to find healing. The most significant act of "pain disposal," though, is asking God for help in forgiving someone else. When we are hurt, we instinctively hold on to our pain, just as the people lined up at the shredder that day held their symbols of disappointment and anger. God alone can help us release our grip on those memories and move on.

THOUGHT

If you were to shred one memory or hurt from the past year, what would it be?

Authentic Relationship

If you are offering your gift at the altar
and there remember that your brother has
something against you, leave your gift
there in front of the altar. First go and be
reconciled to your brother; then come and
offer your gift.

—MATTHEW 5:23–24

It was Communion Sunday, and the pastor was preaching on 1 Corinthians 11—the passage in which the apostle Paul admonishes certain wealthy Corinthians for celebrating the Lord's Supper unworthily by shutting out their poorer brothers and sisters in the faith.

The pastor wanted to make sure his congregation went through a moral inventory before taking the bread and the cup. So to conclude his exhortation, he quoted Matthew 5:23–24 and then said, "Some of you have destroyed a relationship by something you did or said. Even if it might mean missing Communion, God would rather that you get up right now and go into the lobby to call that person and apologize."

In the silence that followed, a large number of people went to the lobby, pulling out their cell phones as they went. The shining looks on their faces as they came back made it clear that they had been through a spiritual bath and were ready to commune with God.

To be authentic in our relationships, we must deal with our failures by confession, repentance, and seeking forgiveness from others. In doing so, we prepare ourselves for deep and loving relationships.

PRAYER

Father, show me ways my relationships could be more authentic through my own confession.

Heart Renovations

> I will give her back her vineyards, and will
> make the Valley of Achor [Trouble] a door
> of hope.
>
> —HOSEA 2:15

Boston's Liberty Hotel boasts luxury accommodations, upscale restaurants, and a celebrity clientele. Guests enjoy more than glamour, however; they also enjoy a glimpse into history.

Built in 1851, the building was once the Charles Street Jail. For 120 years, the building hosted such "guests" as prisoners from a World War II German submarine; the thieves behind the Great Brinks Robbery in 1950; and Frank Abagnale Jr., the con artist portrayed by Leonardo DiCaprio in the movie *Catch Me If You Can.*

Years after being declared unfit for prisoners, the granite building underwent a $150 million renovation. Today the entrance of the former jail is the doorway to a fine Italian restaurant—where guests dine next to original jail bars and brick walls. The catwalks where guards once stood watch are now elegant iron-railing balconies. As one former prisoner said upon visiting the hotel, "How you could take something that was so horrible and turn it into something of tremendous beauty, I don't know."

This is a dim reflection of the transformation God offers us by turning opportunities for punishment in our lives into gateways to restoration. We do the same every time we extend forgiveness to someone who doesn't deserve it. God's justice will not allow him to overlook evil. Yet, in his love, God designed a plan so that the place of justice might become a place of grace.

THOUGHT

Think of someone you harbor anger toward. What would it look like if you allowed your resentment to be transformed into a place of grace?

Part 5

COURTESY

Our Courteous God

Love each other as I have loved you.
—JOHN 15:12

C *ourteous* is not a word we often use to describe God.
Perhaps that's because our concept of courtesy is limited to the idea of being polite. The Greek word that is translated "courtesy" in the New Testament, however, comes from two words, one meaning "friend" and the other meaning "the mind." To be courteous is to think of everyone as a friend—an attitude that God models for us.

When the Israelites were looking for the Promised Land, Moses would go to the tent of meeting where "the LORD would speak to Moses face to face, as a man speaks with his friend" (Exodus 33:11). This tells us that the Creator of the universe wants to be our friend. When Jesus came, he revealed the courtesy of God in all his relationships.

Jesus told the early believers, "I no longer call you servants.… Instead, I have called you friends, for everything that I learned from my Father I have made known to you" (John 15:15).

You might feel distant from God or unsure of what he thinks of you, yet he calls you a friend. He longs for your relationship with him to thrive. He is ready to be your companion and guide, as a true friend loves to be.

Thought

Think for a few moments about the joy of deep friendship. How would thinking of God as a friend change your attitude toward him?

The Least of These

Whatever you did for one of the least
of these…, you did for me.
—MATTHEW 25:40

One of the best ways to develop an attitude of courtesy is to remember that everyone we meet is valuable. For the Christian, this means seeing everyone we meet as a representative of Jesus.

Mother Teresa, founder of the Missionaries of Charity in Calcutta, India, knew this truth well. In fact, it was this reality that motivated her to invest her life in loving people. She once said, "Jesus is the one we take care of, visit, clothe, feed, and comfort.… We should not serve the poor like they *were* Jesus, we should serve the poor because *they are* Jesus."

This attitude is what leads Christians to serve the homeless, help hurricane victims rebuild their homes, and care for the sick. But we are not limited to dramatic events or situations. When we believe that everyone we encounter—whether in public or in our homes—represents Jesus, we want to love them through simple courtesies.

PRAYER

*Jesus, help me remember that when
I love others I am loving you.*

A Snack for the Captors

Love your enemies and pray for those
who persecute you.
—MATTHEW 5:44

Polycarp of Smyrna (AD 69–156) was a leader in the early church. When persecution came to the town of Smyrna, he knew his life was in danger and took refuge on a farm. When the Roman authorities came to arrest him, Polycarp did not respond with anger, fear, or hostility. Instead, "he went downstairs and talked with them.… Straightway he ordered food and drink, as much as they wished, to be set before them at that hour, and he asked them to give him an hour so that he might pray undisturbed.… [H]e stood and prayed—being so filled with the grace of God that for two hours he could not hold his peace, to the amazement of those who heard."

As Polycarp's captors took him back to the city, they tried to persuade him to deny Christ. Polycarp replied, "Eighty-six years I have served him, and he never did me any wrong. How can I blaspheme my King who saved me?" Polycarp was killed for his faith, thanking God that he was counted worthy of suffering.

Polycarp loved the Lord, and he loved the captors who arrested him, even caring for their physical needs and acting courteously in the most difficult circumstances. When Christians are in fellowship with Christ, they can express his love no matter what. The challenge is to live for Christ so that even if we face death, his love will flow through us.

PRAYER

*Dear Father, help me to love you so much
that I am willing to sacrifice anything
to love others as you want me to love them.*

Taking Each Other Seriously

> Are not five sparrows sold for two pennies? Yet not one of them is forgotten by God. Indeed, the very hairs of your head are all numbered. Don't be afraid; you are worth more than many sparrows.
> —LUKE 12:6–7

C. S. Lewis wrote, "There are no *ordinary* people. You have never talked to a mere mortal.... This does not mean that we are to be perpetually solemn. We must play. But our merriment must be of that kind...which exists between people who have, from the outset, taken each other seriously." For the Christian, taking one another seriously means understanding that everyone we encounter—the cranky store clerk, the sullen teenage son, or the employee caught stealing—is made in God's image. Good exists in everyone because we each reflect a good God.

Since God gave his Son so that all who believe in him would have eternal life, we are compelled to join him in loving others, celebrating their worth as God's creation. In light of God's love and sacrifice for every person we meet, how can we fail to treat each one with courtesy?

PRAYER

Lord, forgive me for the times when I have ignored people. Help me today to treat people in a way that recognizes their great worth.

A Time to Give

Mary took about a pint of pure nard, an
expensive perfume; she poured it on
Jesus' feet and wiped his feet with her
hair. And the house was filled with the
fragrance of the perfume.

—JOHN 12:3

Margaret Jensen grew up as the daughter of a pastor
during the Depression. She remembers the day her
family awaited her father's paycheck so they could buy food.
When her father arrived home, he handed her mother not
money but a string of pearls. He bowed low and told his wife,
"Mama.… You have such a beautiful throat, you should wear
pearls."

Margaret's mother graciously accepted the impractical

gift and said she would wear it always. As Margaret writes, "Later she told me, 'There is a time and place for everything. Sometimes we need pearls more than potatoes. That was the time for pearls.'"

Graciously receiving an act of kindness is a way of treating others courteously. When Mary anointed Jesus's feet with expensive perfume, Judas objected. But Jesus said, "Leave her alone.... It was intended that she should save this perfume for the day of my burial" (John 12:5, 7). Mary was the sister of Lazarus, whom Jesus had raised from the dead. Her act was likely an expression of deep appreciation for what Jesus had done. Jesus courteously accepted it and did not question her motive.

Some of us find it easier to give than to receive. But when we show courtesy by receiving what others offer us, we are giving them the opportunity to know the joy of loving.

PRAYER

Father, I pray for the courtesy to
receive the gifts of others well.

Welcoming "Angels"

> Do not forget to entertain strangers, for
> by so doing some people have entertained
> angels without knowing it.
> —HEBREWS 13:2

I can almost picture the elderly Abraham sitting cross-legged in the shade of his tent. He looked past the door flap at the heat shimmering over the Middle Eastern landscape. Were those mirages? No, they were real people. Three visitors were standing near his home.

Custom demanded that Abraham make the strangers welcome, yet he could have reacted in fear or shown hostility rather than hospitality. After all, he had never met these visitors before. But Abraham was the model of courtesy as he bowed, ordered that bread be baked, and then hurried off to see that a calf was cooked to feed the guests (see Genesis 18:1–8).

Do we follow Abraham's example in the art of hospitality? Do we invite people—not just friends, but also acquaintances—over for food and conversation? Do we try to meet the simple needs of the people we run across?

Abraham did not know it at first, but his visitors were heavenly figures: two angels and the Lord himself. Our guests may or may not be angels, but God calls us to show his love to each one.

PRAYER

Lord, remind me to show the courtesy of
hospitality to each person you send my way.

All Are
Welcome Here

The stranger who resides with you shall
be to you as the native among you, and
you shall love him as yourself, for you
were aliens in the land of Egypt; I am the
LORD your God.
        —LEVITICUS 19:34, NASB

The story is told that when the Hindu leader Mohandas
Gandhi was a student in England, he read the New
Testament and became enamored with the life of Christ. He
decided to visit a church where he could ask the pastor how
he might become a Christian. But that conversation never
took place. Gandhi was met at the door by an usher who told

him he was not welcome. Gandhi perceived that the church had its own caste system, and he returned to Hinduism.

Courtesy could have made a world of difference to a young man who would grow up to influence millions. We all know what it's like to go somewhere new and feel like an outsider. Will we be accepted? How are we supposed to act? Yet once we become familiar with the setting, we forget what it was like to feel out of place.

When "outsiders" walk into a church, their speech or way of dress might differ from what is customary. But that is no reason to treat a person discourteously. Every individual is a potential brother or sister in Christ. Seeing each person in that light opens the door to a courteous welcome.

PRAYER

*Father, the next time someone new comes into
my church, home, or place of business,
I want to offer the same welcome you would.*

Redeeming Discourtesy

He who loves a pure heart and whose
speech is gracious will have the king for
his friend.

—PROVERBS 22:11

I didn't know the bank teller well, though I had seen her many times. On this particular occasion I was at the bank to clear up what I perceived to be an overcharge. I explained the situation, and then the teller gave me her perspective, which I felt was in error. So I explained my viewpoint again, using a louder voice. She gave me an answer I didn't want to hear. With an attitude of disgust, I left the bank.

I was angry about how I had been mistreated. Then I

heard God say, *I don't think she could recognize that you are a follower of Jesus.* I confessed my sin to God and received his forgiveness, but I knew I had to return to the bank.

"I came back to apologize to you," I said to the teller. "I feel bad that I took my frustration out on you. You did not deserve that, and I was wrong to have raised my voice. I have already asked God to forgive me, and I want to ask if you will forgive me."

The young woman was quick to offer her forgiveness. I thanked her and said, "I hope the rest of your day will be more pleasant." The next time I was in the bank, I smiled at her, and she smiled back. We had a pleasant conversation.

Courtesy means being willing to apologize when we realize we've been disrespectful. Apologizing and receiving forgiveness not only moves us beyond our actions but also creates a deeper level of friendship.

ACTION STEP

Think about a recent time when you were discourteous to someone. What can you do to restore that relationship?

Thomas Jefferson's Handshake

God does not show favoritism.
—ACTS 10:34

On July 4, 1801, President Thomas Jefferson did the unthinkable at a White House reception: he shook hands with his visitors. His predecessors at the White House, George Washington and John Adams, always bowed to honored guests at official functions. They reserved simple handshakes for less distinguished visitors. By breaking with tradition in how he greeted guests, Jefferson introduced the idea of treating people equally, whatever their social or political standing. Today, politicians shake hands, kiss babies, and greet the public as they would friends, following the pattern that Jefferson established.

Whether politicians treat others as friends because they truly see them that way or because they want to get votes is a legitimate question. Even so, in Jefferson's example we see the value of assuming that everyone around us—whether above or beneath us in social or professional standing—is worthy of friendship. When we welcome people into our lives with a warm smile, a handshake, or kind words, we are showing them the love of God.

THOUGHT

*In what situations do you tend to feel
superior to others? When have you failed
to treat others with courtesy as a result?*

Going Against the Flow

Unlike the culture around you, always
dragging you down to its level of immatu-
rity, God brings the best out of you,
develops well-formed maturity in you.
—ROMANS 12:2, MSG

A coffee shop in Boston posts a sign near the cash regis-
ter that says DON'T DO IT next to a picture of a cell
phone with a red line through it. The coffee shop manager
says the sign has cut down on the number of people who
hold up the line while finishing a phone conversation before—
or while—placing their orders.

Common courtesies have become so *un*common that

many companies now hire "etiquette experts" to teach social graces in the workplace. Employers see that disrespectful attitudes and actions reduce productivity and hurt morale. They want to make changes, such as prohibiting text-messaging in meetings. Simple etiquette reminders reflect a personal and professional respect that help people build stronger relationships.

The lack of courtesy in our society gives us more of an opportunity to stand out as loving people. The Greek word *ekklesia* is the word most commonly translated "church" in the New Testament. It literally means "called-out ones." It describes people who have responded to the love of God and have been called out to become followers of Christ. Being called out means making the choice to love others in every-day ways. In the workplace and at home, courtesy is as simple as treating others with respect.

ACTION STEP

What is one habit you have that shows disrespect for others? What can you do this week to change that habit?

"Excuse Me..."

Jesus traveled about from one town and
village to another, proclaiming the good
news of the kingdom of God.

—LUKE 8:1

One of the most difficult times to be courteous is when
others interrupt us. How many of us have sighed
inwardly when a co-worker "pops in just for a minute" when
we are trying to prepare for a meeting? Even if we need to tell
someone we are busy at the moment, we can do so courteously.

One day Jesus was walking with a huge crowd surround-
ing him when a woman touched his cloak. He might well
have been tired, hungry, and eager to reach his destination.
To stop just then would only delay him, by human standards.
Yet he stopped and asked, "Who touched me?" (Luke 8:45).

He then identified the woman in need of healing and commended her. "Daughter, your faith has healed you. Go in peace" (verse 48).

On the same occasion, a man named Jairus fell at Jesus's feet, asking him to come to his house because his daughter was dying. Jesus changed his plans and stopped by Jairus's house, where he raised the girl from the dead.

By focusing more on God's "to-do" list than his own, Jesus showed that he viewed people not as interruptions but as friends.

PRAYER

Lord, I want to be so aware of your purposes
for my life that I treat even interruptions
as opportunities to love others.

Love in Chicago

This is how much God loved the world: He
gave his Son, his one and only Son. And this
is why: so that no one need be destroyed; by
believing in him, anyone can have a whole and
lasting life. God didn't go to all the trouble of
sending his Son merely to point an accusing
finger, telling the world how bad it was. He
came to help, to put the world right again.
—JOHN 3:16–17, MSG

D. L. Moody was a nineteenth-century evangelist who
influenced millions through his preaching and publishing. His public ministry began in the 1850s when he
preached to sailors in Chicago's port and to gamblers at nearby
saloons. Then on a trip to Ireland, Moody met a converted

pickpocket from Lancashire, England, by the name of Harry Moorhouse. Moody was not greatly impressed with the frail young man but allowed Moorhouse to preach in Moody's absence when the Englishman visited Chicago in 1868.

Moorhouse preached seven straight nights on the love of God as told in John 3:16. When Moody returned to town and found Moorhouse drawing listeners to God with the power of his message, Moody was greatly moved. He recognized that his own preaching had proclaimed that God hates sin *and* the sinner. Moody was convicted of his sin of ungraciousness and determined to alter his message from then on, making it more reflective of God's love.

When we welcome others in love, no matter what they have done, we demonstrate the love of God—a love that changes lives.

Thought

*Does your spiritual community treat people
as though God loves them no matter
what they have done? Do you?*

Part 6

HUMILITY

The Humble King

Who is like the LORD our God, the One
who sits enthroned on high, who stoops
down to look on the heavens and the earth?
—PSALM 113:5–6

Imagine that it is late afternoon on the first day a human
had walked on earth. The God who had just made stars,
water, and trees does something remarkable: he begins a conversation with the first human. In talking with Adam, God
demonstrates that he is a God who bows low to be with his
creation. Later, when Adam and Eve turn against him, God
searches for them (see Genesis 3:8), again humbling himself
to be with his children.

We rarely think of God as humble. *High, holy, exalted,*

yes, but not *humble*. Yet from the beginning of creation, God has stooped to relate to us because he loves us so much.

We see the ultimate display of God's humility in Christ. When the Son of God took his place among us, he "made himself nothing, taking the very nature of a servant, being made in human likeness" (Philippians 2:7). Christ stepped down so that we could step up. He took less so that we could have more. This kind of humility grows out of a heart that genuinely loves others and wants to help them succeed. And so, as we love others, we remain close to the God who humbly stays by our side.

PRAYER

*Lord, I worship you for your greatness
and for bowing low to be with me.*

Jesus's Eyes

[God] told me, "My grace is enough; it's all
you need. My strength comes into its own
in your weakness." Once I heard that, I
was glad to let it happen. I quit focusing
on the handicap and began appreciating
the gift. It was a case of Christ's strength
moving in on my weakness.… And so the
weaker I get, the stronger I become.

—2 CORINTHIANS 12:9–10, MSG

L ilias Trotter, missionary to the Muslims of Algeria, tells
the story of a young girl named Melha, who understood
the essence of humility.

"[Melha] went right up to her nearly blind father and

pointed to one of the pictures on the wall—one of the Lord calling a little child to Him—and said, 'Look at Jesus.'

" 'I have no eyes, O my daughter—I cannot see,' was the answer. [The girl] lifted her head and eyes to the picture and said, 'O Jesus, look at father!' "

Had Melha shown the pride of adulthood, she might have agreed with her father that it was useless to try to see God. But in joyful humility, she simply acknowledged that her father was weak and God was strong. She knew that God sees us before we can even look at him. He longs for us to acknowledge how dependent we are on him.

In our ambition we believe that we must get our lives together before we can turn to God. But in our humility we realize that only through God will we find the completeness we need to love him, see him, and care for others.

PRAYER

God, I am weak today.
Help me to be strong in you.

For the Good of Others

You know the grace of our Lord Jesus
Christ, that though he was rich, yet for
your sakes he became poor, so that you
through his poverty might become rich.
—2 CORINTHIANS 8:9

B orn into a noble family, Domingo de Guzmán
(1170–1221), founder of the Dominicans, was known
for self-sacrifice and caring for others. As a teenager, Domingo
was an excellent scholar, and his books were prized possessions. Even so, he had a greater love: caring for the needy.

Domingo believed that others would know love "by an
example of humility and other virtues far more readily than

by any external display or verbal battles." So the priest from a prestigious family chose to live the life of poverty. He began by traveling barefoot and refusing to sleep on a bed in favor of the ground. He accepted discomfort as an opportunity to praise God.

Domingo sacrificed material treasures because he knew human lives were worth more than his possessions. He sacrificed status because he knew showing love to others was more important than being applauded. Humility allowed him to see a greater good and act on it.

Setting an example of humility is a way of loving others. Being humble might mean sacrificing money, a promotion, or our culture's most prized possession—time. When we understand that all good things are gifts from God, we are free to give them up for the good of others.

PRAYER

Father, help me to see how sacrificing my
own comfort can be a way of loving others.

Getting Out of the Way

He must become greater; I must become less.
—JOHN 3:30

We've seen it happen many times. A leader's messages get large numbers of people stirred up, and it seems like he's the head of a great movement of God. But as the auditorium seats fill up week after week and the TV ratings skyrocket, something happens. He gets full of himself. It's less about God and more about him. Self-indulgence and sin are only a step away, and suddenly the nightly news is chronicling his fall.

That was *not* the way it was with John the Baptist, a preacher who attained the popularity of a rock star two thousand years ago. As rustic as was John's appearance (wearing an animal-skin robe), as challenging as was his message ("Repent!"), and as inconvenient as was his location (the desert), the people loved John. "The whole Judean countryside and all the people of Jerusalem went out to him" (Mark 1:5). Many wondered if he might be the Messiah (see Luke 3:15).

John never let others' expectations carry him away. He knew that his God-given role was to point to Christ (see Mark 1:7). He got out of the way so Jesus, not John, could be glorified.

Prayer

Help me learn to get out of the way, Lord, so that others (especially you!) might be more easily seen.

Driving to Connecticut

Follow the example of Christ.
—1 CORINTHIANS 11:1

Ellen works as an administrative assistant in a junior high school in North Carolina. She is known as an efficient worker with a genuine interest in students. What many do not know is that each Tuesday night Ellen goes to the city jail and leads a Bible study for female inmates. Over the years, many of these women have experienced the love of Christ through Ellen.

When Ashley, one of the women Ellen met at the jail, was transferred to a prison in Connecticut, Ellen wanted to help her however she could. Ellen had met Ashley's mother, who moved to North Carolina after her Florida home was destroyed in a hurricane. Knowing how much Ashley and her mom wanted to see each other, Ellen drove the mother to Connecticut a few weeks after Ashley had been transferred there.

Being willing to use your vacation days to help an elderly mother spend time with her daughter speaks loudly of humility. Ellen put her own needs aside for the sake of lifting up someone else.

Humility calls us to reach out to others in the same way Christ reached out to people. That means being aware of the needs of others and seizing opportunities to meet those needs.

ACTION STEP

Give up something this week so you can help meet the practical needs of someone outside your family.

Hard to Ignore

Come to me, all you who are weary and
burdened, and I will give you rest. Take
my yoke upon you and learn from me,
for I am gentle and humble in heart, and
you will find rest for your souls.
—MATTHEW 11:28–29

Friedrich Nietzsche (1844–1900) believed the goal of
human existence was the cultivation of individuals who
towered above the herd. His philosophy of the Superman was
the polar opposite of a self-giving God. Yet in the final years
of his life, Nietzsche signed his letters "the Crucified One,"
still wrestling with how to respond to the Christ of the Bible.
The philosopher who pronounced God dead found it impossible to ignore the humility of Jesus.

It's easy to minimize the remarkable choice God made when he came to earth not as a king or a warrior but as a baby. God knew that humility, more than a show of power, would get our attention. How else would we come to believe that the road to greatness leads downward?

Humility remains a key part of how God shows his love. That's why he desires to see this characteristic reproduced in his children. On at least three occasions, Jesus repeated the principle, "Everyone who exalts himself will be humbled, and he who humbles himself will be exalted" (Luke 14:11; 18:14; see also Matthew 23:12). Christ's words echoed the life he was living—a life so surprising in its humility that it is hard for anyone to ignore.

PRAYER

Lord, I want to have such a servant's heart in the way I relate to others that I surprise people.

The Wisdom of Children

Unless you change and become like little children, you will never enter the kingdom of heaven. Therefore, whoever humbles himself like this child is the greatest in the kingdom of heaven.

—MATTHEW 18:3–4

Author Kim Bolton faced a morning of laundry, dirty dishes, and carpool responsibilities. As she carried another basket of clothes to the laundry room, she heard her two-year-old son's tiny voice. "Hey, Mom. Why dontcha come and sit wif me in da big chair?"

Kim explained that she had so much to do that she

couldn't sit down. "Just a wittle minute," her son asked again, patting the space next to him.

Kim dropped her laundry and sat down.

"Now, isn't dis nice, Mom?"

Mother and son sat together for a total of ninety seconds. Then the child patted Kim's knee and said, "You can go now." Kim returned to the demands of the day with a more peaceful pace.

Jesus says we must humble ourselves as little children if we are to enter the kingdom of heaven. Becoming as children means that in the midst of busy days we allow ourselves to be open to moments of building relationships instead of getting things done. When we discover the humility of a child, we step down from the throne of self-reliance and bow before God. In humility we acknowledge that it's not all up to us after all.

ACTION STEP

Think about a circumstance or task that
feels overwhelming to you right now.
What would it look like today to trust Jesus
with that situation as a child would?

A Radical Idea

He has showed you, O man, what is
good. And what does the LORD require
of you? To act justly and to love mercy
and to walk humbly with your God.
—MICAH 6:8

As heir to the Borden Dairy estate, William Borden was
a millionaire by the time he graduated from high
school. While a student at Yale University, Borden was president of Phi Beta Kappa and was active in football, baseball,
crew, and wrestling. But his passion was his religious work,
particularly the rescue mission he established.

By the time Borden finished Yale in 1909, he had decided to become a missionary to China despite warnings
from his friends that he was wasting his life. He enrolled in

Princeton Seminary and traveled to other colleges and seminaries, urging students to give their lives to missions. Through all of his other commitments, he kept up his visits to the Yale Hope Mission and gave generously to support its ministry.

Borden died at the age of twenty-five while training in Egypt, but his influence lives on. As Princeton professor Charles Erdman said of Borden, "Apart from Christ, there is no explanation of such a life."

True humility doesn't make sense in human terms. Giving up a privileged life to serve others is nothing less than a radical idea. Indeed, apart from the humility God models for us, there is no explanation for it at all.

PRAYER

Father, I want to live my life in a way
that doesn't make sense apart from you.

The Worst Kind of Pride

I'm not saying that I have this all together, that I have it made. But I am well on my way, reaching out for Christ, who has so wondrously reached out for me. Friends, don't get me wrong: By no means do I count myself an expert in all of this, but I've got my eye on the goal, where God is beckoning us onward—to Jesus.

—PHILIPPIANS 3:12–14, MSG

I was reluctant to start a work that I felt God was calling me to do," an acquaintance told me. "I had no training and felt I would make a fool of myself. Then a friend said to me, 'God does not always call the equipped, but he always equips the called.' So I stepped out and God did the rest." When this woman trusted God with the outcome, she was set free to serve others.

If you feel unable or unworthy to attempt something for God, consider whether it is an unhealthy desire to do things perfectly that holds you back. As author Warren Wiersbe said, "Denying that we can accomplish God's work is not humility; it is the worst kind of pride." If you are waiting until you become better, brighter, or more ready, you are probably relying on yourself more than God.

The apostle Paul knew that following Christ's call in his life would sometimes be a messy process. As he wrote, "Not that I...have already been made perfect, but I press on to take hold of that for which Christ Jesus took hold of me" (Philippians 3:12). When your greatest desire is to love others as Christ leads, you practice the humility that is needed to risk making mistakes.

THOUGHT

Think of one thing you feel called to do that you have hesitated to begin. Pray about whether God is telling you to wait or you are holding back because you are afraid of failing.

Servant Leadership

[Jesus] poured water into a basin and
began to wash his disciples' feet, drying
them with the towel that was wrapped
around him.

—JOHN 13:5

I once knew a pastor who was rising in popularity in his
denomination. He was invited to serve on various boards
and committees and to speak at national gatherings. I watched
him closely and never saw a spirit of pride. He simply sought
to do his best when he was asked to serve.

On one occasion when this man was asked to speak at a
statewide meeting for pastors, he recommended that one of

his young associate ministers speak instead. He felt that the younger pastors needed to be heard. I've spent a lot of time with pastors. I can tell you, this is not the normal attitude of a pastor who is at the midpoint of his career. I saw this man's action as a sign of genuine humility: the desire to step down so others may step up.

When leaders have true humility, they aren't concerned about exalting themselves. Instead, they help younger leaders find their place in the kingdom. If leaders walk the road of humility, there's a good chance that others will follow. As Jesus taught, true greatness is seen in those who serve others.

ACTON STEP

Think of someone who would have an opportunity to take on a leadership role or particular responsibility, if you would take action on his or her behalf. Ask God how he might want you to serve that person.

Bread of Peace

Blessed are the peacemakers, for they will
be called sons of God. Blessed are those
who are persecuted because of righteousness, for theirs is the kingdom of heaven.
—MATTHEW 5:9–10

In 1938, 250 men were huddled in a small Russian prison
cell. A man named David Braun was among them. He
soon noticed that an Orthodox priest shared the cell. Although the old man's face radiated peace, two other men
mocked him and blasphemed what was holy to him. He
responded with gentleness.

One day when David received a parcel of bread from his
wife, he gave the priest some of the bread. Instead of eating
it, however, the priest broke the bread and gave it to the two

men who had taunted him. David never heard mockery in the cell again. Though the priest died soon after, his humble spirit continued to influence others.

Humility doesn't worry about slights or ridicule. That doesn't mean that rejection causes us no pain. In fact, it is when our efforts are mocked that humility is most difficult— and most needed. We have to rely on God's help, believing that he understands far more than we do the goodness and the risk of loving others.

Thought

Think about times when the opinions of others have prevented you from loving others in humility. Ask God for the humility that transcends your circumstances.

Pocket Change

Show proper respect to everyone.
—1 PETER 2:17

Robert Goodwin, president of the Points of Light Foundation, tells of passing a homeless man while on the way to work one winter morning. Goodwin had seen the man many times before and often gave him money. When he passed the man that particular day, however, he found that he had no change in his pocket. Instead of continuing on to work, Goodwin said to the man: "I'm sorry, my brother. I don't have anything to give today."

At that, the man responded: "Oh, but you already did. You called me brother."

Goodwin knew his place in society was more "acceptable" than the homeless man's. But he chose a different standard—

a standard that affirms everyone as an equal under God. He acted on the belief that someone else's needs are just as important as one's own. In stopping to call this man his brother, Goodwin sacrificed a bit of time, but more importantly, he sacrificed the right to be more important than someone else. He showed true humility: a peacefulness of heart that affirms the value of those around us.

Prayer

Every time I encounter a stranger today, Lord,
help me to see him or her as you do.

Part 7

GENEROSITY

Cooperating with God

God is able to make all grace abound to
you, so that in all things at all times, having
all that you need, you will abound in every
good work.

—2 Corinthians 9:8

David Livingstone, the great missionary and African
explorer, once wrote, "I will place no value on anything I have or may possess, except in relation to the kingdom of Christ. If anything will advance the interests of that
kingdom, it shall be given or kept, only as by giving or keeping of it I shall most promote the glory of Him to whom I
owe all my hopes in time and eternity." Livingstone knew

that all we have—and most importantly who we *are*—are gifts from God. By giving time, energy, abilities, and money, we cooperate with God in establishing his kingdom.

When the demands of life make serving God seem overwhelming, it's a sign that we're trusting in ourselves rather than in God. We reason that if only we had a little *more* time or money, we could serve God and give to his kingdom. Yet Jesus said, "Whoever can be trusted with very little can also be trusted with much" (Luke 16:10).

God knows our needs and the pressures we face. In the midst of that, he says: *I love you so much that I long for you to join with me in what I am doing.* Giving is not a matter of how *much* we have; it is a matter of loving God with *what* we have.

PRAYER

Father, I want to share what you have given me
so I can be a part of what you are doing. Thank
you for using what I have for your kingdom.

One Percent More

Each man should give what he has decided
in his heart to give, not reluctantly or under
compulsion, for God loves a cheerful giver.
—2 CORINTHIANS 9:7

A recent conversation with a friend reminded me of the
joy we find in giving. "When my wife and I were married," he said, "we decided to give 10 percent of our income
to the Lord's work. By the end of our first year of marriage, I
had started a little business and God had blessed us. I said to
my wife, 'As believers in Christ who have received so much
from him, I feel like we should do more. Would you be willing for us to give 11 percent of our income next year?' My
wife agreed.

"At the end of that year, God had blessed our business,

and I asked my wife if she would be willing to give 12 percent the following year. Again she agreed. After that, every year we added 1 percent more of our total income to our giving, and every year, at the end of the year, we had more left over than we did the year before."

"How long have you been married?" I asked.

He smiled and said, "Forty-nine years." It didn't take me long to calculate that this couple was now giving 59 percent of their income to the causes of Christ. As I think of my friend's smile, I am reminded that joyful, generous giving is one of the ways we express our love to God.

ACTION STEP

Revisit your giving plan and consider whether God would have you increase the amount by 1 percent of your total income.

Prayer List

[Anna] was a widow until she was eighty-
four. She never left the temple but wor-
shiped night and day, fasting and praying.
—LUKE 2:37

I recently visited one of the elderly members of our church. She said to me, "I'm at a stage in life when I cannot do much physically to help others. So God has given me the ministry of prayer. I spend two hours a day praying for others."

This woman prays for fifteen minutes on the hour from 8:00 a.m. until 11:00 a.m. and from 1:00 p.m. to 4:00 p.m. She showed me her prayer notebook, listing the names of those she prays for. The list included all of her extended family, many in her church family, missionaries, neighbors in her community, and former co-workers. She adds to her list the individuals who call her with prayer requests.

At this point in this godly woman's life, prayer is the way she can generously love others to the fullest. And what a contribution she is making to the kingdom of God! When I left that day, I made sure that my name was added to her prayer notebook.

PRAYER

Father, when I think I have nothing to offer to you or others, remind me of what I can give.

Good Gifts

Every good and perfect gift is from
above, coming down from the Father
of the heavenly lights, who does not
change like shifting shadows.
—JAMES 1:17

I have always found it astounding that the eternal God
would invite us to ask him for gifts, but that is precisely
what Jesus taught. Knowing that God delights in giving good
things to his children, Jesus encouraged his followers to ask.
"Which of you, if his son asks for bread, will give him a
stone? Or if he asks for a fish, will give him a snake? If you,
then, though you are evil, know how to give good gifts to
your children, how much more will your Father in heaven
give good gifts to those who ask him!" (Matthew 7:9–11).

God is the great Gift Giver. Throughout history, he has revealed himself as One who expresses his love by giving to his children. God's gifts have nothing to do with how we "perform." They are reflections of his pure love, which is freely given to us.

Following God's example, when we are generous to others, our gifts are not based on the other person's actions. When we give to others, we reflect the love of a heavenly Father who delights in giving to those he loves.

THOUGHT

*What good gift is within your power
to give to someone who needs it today?*

Giving Your Life Away

Greater love has no one than this, that
he lay down his life for his friends.
—JOHN 15:13

On April 16, 2007, a gunman went on a killing rampage across the campus of Virginia Tech. In Norris Hall, students in Professor Liviu Librescu's classroom heard gunfire and shouting from the next classroom. Librescu, a seventy-seven-year-old Holocaust survivor, told his students to escape through the classroom windows while he braced himself against the door. As students dropped to the ground outside, the professor held the door shut against the gunman. Then a bullet came through the door and took his life.

Jesus taught that the ultimate act of generosity is to give up one's life for someone else. He set the example when he gave his life to save us. As we act out his love, we will be ready to give ourselves to others. That might mean sacrificing our lives, as Librescu did. It might mean setting aside our plans in order to care for someone in need. It might mean offering what is most precious to us so that we can embrace what is most precious to God.

When we learn how God wants us to love others, we will "lay down" our lives daily by giving ourselves in self-sacrificing love.

Prayer

Lord, I want to be ready to give even my life to love others. Help me know how to start loving others with that level of generosity.

A Delightful Land

Give, and it will be given to you. A good
measure, pressed down, shaken together
and running over, will be poured into
your lap. For with the measure you use,
it will be measured to you.

—LUKE 6:38

I n *The Pilgrim's Progress,* John Bunyan wrote: "A man there
was, though some did count him mad, the more he cast
away the more he had." When we learn the grace of giving,
God gives us abundantly more in return.

God spoke this truth to ancient Israel: " 'Bring the whole
tithe into the storehouse, that there may be food in my

house. Test me in this,' says the LORD Almighty, 'and see if I will not throw open the floodgates of heaven and pour out so much blessing that you will not have room enough for it.… Then all the nations will call you blessed, for yours will be a delightful land,' says the LORD Almighty" (Malachi 3:10, 12).

Generosity comes not from a desire to be rewarded but from genuine love for others. It is a spiritual paradox that when we give away what God gives us, we open ourselves to receive more blessing from God. We also point others to the "delightful land" that can be found through following God (verse 12).

PRAYER

Lord, I don't want to hoard what you have given me. May people come to love you because they see your love expressed generously through me.

Willing to Sacrifice

> We want you to know about the grace that
> God has given the Macedonian churches. Out
> of the most severe trial, their overflowing joy
> and their extreme poverty welled up in rich
> generosity. For I testify that they gave as much
> as they were able, and even beyond their ability.
> —2 CORINTHIANS 8:1–3

E very Christmas the church where I serve receives a special offering for missions of mercy overseas. A few years ago I challenged the congregation in January to consider setting aside twenty dollars per week beyond their tithe. At the end of the year each family would be able to give one thousand dollars to the missions offering.

A number of people accepted the challenge, and our

missions offering that year exceeded five hundred thousand dollars. One young couple told me: "We had only been married six months when you threw out your challenge.... We set aside twenty dollars each week. Several times we were tempted to dip into our missions offering, but we resisted. It is with great joy that we give our thousand dollars to missions." They handed me an envelope containing fifty twenty-dollar bills.

Financial planners advise setting aside a little more money than you think you can afford when you save for retirement. The same principle is true of giving, though with different reasons in mind. Your level of giving should affect the choices you make about other expenditures. If it doesn't, you might consider giving more than you think you can spare.

The envelope I received from the young couple represented sacrifice—joyful, pleasing sacrifice to the Giver of all good gifts.

THOUGHT

When was the last time you sacrificed
something to give to someone else?
What could you sacrifice today?

A Church
That Cares

Dear children, let us not love with words
or tongue but with actions and in truth.
—1 JOHN 3:18

If generosity became a way of life for the church you attend, what might it look like? Widows, single parents, and children of divorce would benefit from love that is expressed in practical and relational ways. Programs would focus on bringing the healing message of Christ to broken hearts. Every parishioner would feel valued for his or her gifts and encouraged to use those gifts. New ministries would develop as members saw opportunities for expressing love to those in need.

A few years ago the church where I serve began to explore ways we could love our city more effectively. We now provide weekend snacks to elementary schoolchildren who live in an impoverished neighborhood. In the fall we provide backpacks and school supplies to the same students. Other church members minister to local prisoners and their families.

At a growing church I visited in Arkansas, members created a career-link workshop to train and assist the unemployed and underemployed. Classes focused on résumé preparation, job-interview skills, career-path planning, budgeting, job-search strategies, and overcoming employment barriers. Then the church got creative about other ways to give—grilling hot dogs at an apartment complex, delivering lunches to kids, helping elderly neighbors with home maintenance.

When a church chooses to be generous in loving others, the opportunities are unlimited.

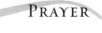

PRAYER

*Lord, help me to be a part of making my
church community known for its generosity.*

Fundraising for Famine Victims

> You will be made rich in every way so that
> you can be generous on every occasion,
> and through us your generosity will result
> in thanksgiving to God.
> —2 CORINTHIANS 9:11

A series of drier-than-usual years pushes an arid nation over the brink of famine. Fields lie cracked under the sun. Parents sit with heads in hands, despairing over not being able to provide for their families. Malnourished children wander about on stick legs. A call goes out to the churches to send financial assistance.

This scenario might play out in many countries today.

The event I have in mind, however, was the famine that occurred in Israel during the mid to late 40s. When Paul and Barnabas made an initial famine-relief visit to Jerusalem in AD 46 (see Acts 11:29–30), the Jerusalem church expressed the hope that Gentile believers would continue to help. Paul made a special appeal for funds, even giving the church at Corinth advice about raising money (see 1 Corinthians 16:1–4). In his next letter, he urged them to complete their gift (see 2 Corinthians 8–9). Paul taught Christians to give regularly, proportionately, and cheerfully. The collection effort was completed in AD 57, and the funds were delivered by Paul and a group of delegates chosen by the contributing Gentile churches.

Every time we give our money to help others, we are standing in an ancient Christian tradition of sharing God's love through generosity.

PRAYER

Father, when I receive appeals for financial assistance, show me how you want me to give.

Diamonds in the Rough

How great is the love the Father has
lavished on us, that we should be called
children of God!

—1 JOHN 3:1

Janet has taught girls in Sunday school for many years.
Eight years ago she realized that her girls needed more
than she could give in one hour on Sunday morning, so she
started bringing them to her home on Saturdays. She pro-
vides lunch, has a Bible study, and teaches the girls life skills.

"These are children from single-parent homes, from fos-
ter homes, and sometimes from abusive homes," Janet told
me. "We teach them table etiquette, telephone etiquette, how

to care for themselves, and how to study." Janet occasionally brings in other people to address such issues as abuse and eating disorders. "We're making a difference in the girls' lives," she said.

Janet is following in the footsteps of Jesus, who ate and walked and conversed with those he loved. She also follows in the steps of Paul the apostle, who invested time with young Timothy (see 2 Timothy 2:2). For two thousand years, the love of Christ has been expressed to others by giving away hours of the day.

It's a spirit of generosity that frees Janet to care for those she calls "diamonds in the rough." She could be doing many other things on Saturday mornings, but she knows that she can't deeply influence the lives of her girls without spending time with them.

PRAYER

Lord, I know I hold time too tightly some-times. Help me realize when I need to loosen my grip so I will be free to help others.

Pulling One
Off for God

To each one the manifestation of the
Spirit is given for the common good.
—1 CORINTHIANS 12:7

A staple of any good caper movie is a team of people who combine their specialties to pull off the caper—usually a bank robbery or jewel heist. A typical team might include the strategist, the insider, the explosives expert, the technology wonk, and the getaway driver.

Something like this assemblage of gifted individuals takes place in the church. But the "caper" we are trying to pull off is loving people. The Holy Spirit gives spiritual gifts to the followers of Jesus so that the church is stocked with apostles, prophets, teachers, evangelists, and others—all of whom, when they combine their abilities under the leadership of the Spirit, help show God's love to the world.

When we're sitting in a movie theater, it's easy to see how one person's absence could ruin a caper. Yet when sitting in church, we sometimes forget how valuable each person's contributions are to the kingdom of God. The truth is, when you or I fail to use our gifts, the entire body suffers. God gives us gifts "for the common good." One of the greatest joys of the Christian life is to share those gifts generously and see how God uses our contributions for the benefit of others.

THOUGHT

What are your spiritual gifts, and where are your gifts needed in the work of the church?

A Hitchhiker's Guide to Generosity

> "I tell you the truth," [Jesus] said, "this poor widow has put in more than all the others. All these people gave their gifts out of their wealth; but she out of her poverty put in all she had to live on."
>
> —LUKE 21:3–4

Author Sebastian Junger was hitchhiking through Wyoming when a disheveled man carrying a lunch box asked if Junger had food. "Clearly he didn't have any," recalled Junger, "and if I admitted that I did, he'd ask for some.... Twenty years later I still remember my answer: 'I got some cheese.'

" 'You won't make it to California with just a little cheese,' he said. 'You'll starve.' " Junger began to understand. This man was offering *him* food. Though Junger protested, the man gave him a sandwich, an apple, and a bag of chips.

"I learned a lot of things in college, I thought.... But I had to stand out there on that frozen piece of interstate to learn true generosity from a homeless man."

We can learn great things about love in the least likely places. Those who possess little might teach us the most about giving. Perhaps that is because the neediest know best of all the importance of small acts of generosity.

Each of us has the potential to love others well. So when generosity shows up in unusual places, don't be surprised. God might want to show you that he's ready to give good gifts when you least expect them.

PRAYER

Dear God, forgive me for the times when
I have rejected someone else's generosity
because it came from an unexpected source.

Part 8

HONESTY

Living in the Real World

Take on an entirely new way of life—a God-fashioned life, a life renewed from the inside and working itself into your conduct as God accurately reproduces his character in you. What this adds up to, then, is this: no more lies, no more pretense.

—EPHESIANS 4:22–25, MSG

As a teenager, Daniel Taylor asked a speaker at a Christian camp about a moral issue that was bothering him. Instead of pointing out what was right and wrong, the speaker said, "You need to decide at what plane you are going to live your life."

The words had a great impact on the teenager. Now he asks himself and his children, "On what plane are you going to live your life?... Are you going to waver here, rationalize there, indulge yourself in this, temporarily suspend your convictions over that?"

Dishonesty is one of the most subtle forms of unloving behavior. How many of us have told small lies to rationalize our behavior? How many of us make daily compromises instead of acting on and speaking the whole truth?

Taylor concludes, "The real world is God's world, not the poor, perverted imitation world with which most people are satisfied. To live as fully as possible in that real world, you have to decide if you want to live on that high plane."

Every time we speak truth when it seems easier to lie, we come more fully alive in Christ. We show that no matter what is acceptable in our society, we want to make a choice that is far more satisfying than anything a deceptive world can offer.

Thought

On what plane are you going to live your life?

Creating a Masterpiece

Whoever lives by the truth comes into the
light, so that it may be seen plainly that
what he has done has been done through
God.

—JOHN 3:21

Some art experts estimate that forgeries make up nearly
half of the art market. Deception is so prevalent that art
dealers are encouraged to attend private exhibitions of forged
works so they can learn what to watch for when buying and
selling paintings.

Just as forgeries in the art world hurt genuine works, so
our false words hurt our genuine efforts at loving others.

When we give in to falsehood, we damage not only our relationships but also our thought life and sense of purpose. Paul writes, "Tell your neighbor the truth. In Christ's body we're all connected to each other, after all. When you lie to others, you end up lying to yourself" (Ephesians 4:25, MSG).

Of course, telling the truth is not always easy, any more than creating a genuine work of art is easy. Sometimes lying seems safer, because it promises a quick escape from what could otherwise be an awkward situation. We opt for a lie because we want to protect our fragile egos from what others might say or think if they knew what we really were like. But building a habit of truth telling leads to genuine relationships. It creates a masterpiece that we will never have to fear showing to anyone.

PRAYER

Father, teach me to speak in such a way
that no one need ever wonder whether my
words are a forgery of the truth.

Glorious Mystery

[Keep] a clear conscience, so that those who
speak maliciously against your good behavior
in Christ may be ashamed of their slander.
—1 PETER 3:16

Fuller Theological Seminary's School of Intercultural
Studies conducted a survey among 750 Muslims who
had converted to Christianity. The survey showed that the
strongest motivating factor behind conversion was seeing
Christians practice what they preached.

The results of this survey and others like it are both an
encouragement and a challenge. God gives us the privilege of
seeing our lifestyle make a difference to others. Christian
integrity means representing God well, speaking his truth
and his love. If that seems hard to do, it is—on our own. Yet

Christ, "the hope of glory," is in us to love others as Jesus would love them. Paul describes this as a mystery that is too glorious to understand (see Colossians 1:27).

Living with integrity is one of the most important things we can do to draw others to Jesus. That doesn't mean we live perfect lives. We will fail, and we'll need to ask forgiveness of God and others. But even in our failings, we can reflect an authenticity that leads others to a perfect God.

Thought

In the last week, when has your behavior not lived up to the values you profess?

Gossip-Free Zone

> Do not let any unwholesome talk come out
> of your mouths, but only what is helpful for
> building others up according to their needs,
> that it may benefit those who listen.
> —Ephesians 4:29

Sam Chapman (no relation of mine) worked at an office where people stated the facts—but rarely with kindness. The gossip was so bad that morale suffered and careers were ruined. So when Chapman founded his own company, he banned gossip completely. The rule is: if you gossip, you get fired. It took time for employees to adjust, but now they value the honesty that a gossip-free environment creates.

Dishonesty, deception, and exaggeration hurt relationships. We might be telling the truth *about* someone but forgetting that honesty incorporates all seven characteristics of a loving person. Gossip is never kind, patient, forgiving, courteous, humble, or generous. And it can keep us from speaking the truth in a loving way directly to the person who needs to hear it. If our words don't build up a person, they are best left unspoken.

The writer of Proverbs tells us, "The tongue has the power of life and death" (18:21). As we draw close to God, we become more aware of the times when we speak honestly but not lovingly. Whether or not we live or work in a gossip-free zone, we will learn to love others with our words as we view our relationships in light of our relationship with God.

PRAYER

Before I speak about someone else, Lord,
remind me to ask myself if what I am
about to say is both true and loving.

Just You and God

> Obey your earthly masters in everything;
> and do it, not only when their eye is on you
> and to win their favor, but with sincerity of
> heart and reverence for the Lord.
> —COLOSSIANS 3:22

In the 1980s it came to the attention of the IRS that large numbers of taxpayers were claiming unauthorized dependents. Some claims were ridiculous (such as Fluffy, who probably had four legs), and some were understandable (divorced spouses both claiming their children). In 1986, Congress passed a law requiring taxpayers to list their dependent children's Social Security numbers. When the returns came in the following April, seven million dependents had disappeared.

Challenging taxpayers to verify their claims generated nearly $3 billion in additional tax revenue just in the first year.

It has been said that a gentleman is one who uses the butter knife when he is alone. Who are you when no one is looking? Some people would never lie to a friend but don't hesitate to cheat an employer or the government. Yet dishonesty in one area of life leads to dishonesty in other areas.

It's easy to slip into dishonest living when we're convinced we won't get caught. But just as dishonesty hurts our earthly relationships, so it hurts our relationship with God. He is a loving Father who wants a genuine relationship with his children. A key part of our relationship with him, as in any relationship, is to be true in our words, thoughts, and actions.

PRAYER

Forgive me for my "secret" dishonesty, Lord. Help me have integrity whether I'm with others or alone with you.

Taking Off the Goatskins

Your brother came deceitfully and took
your blessing.
—Genesis 27:35

Jacob's name means "deceiver," and he certainly lived up to
his name. He deceived his brother, Esau, and his father,
Isaac, to grab the rights of the firstborn even though he was
the younger son.

Jacob took advantage of Esau's hunger one day to extort
a promise that Esau would give up his birthright. Next, Jacob
took advantage of Isaac's blindness to pretend to be Esau
and receive the older son's blessing. Jacob must have looked
ridiculous standing there wearing goatskins so he would feel

hairy to the touch—like Esau. But the result of Jacob's deceit was not ridiculous; it was serious indeed. He caused breaches between himself and his father and brother that never were entirely healed.

Jacob had allowed resentment to build against his brother—and allowed doubt about God's blessing to grow in his mind. Craig Barnes writes that Jacob "has resented Esau for so long that he has damaged his ability to be himself."

Are you trying to be someone you are not because you don't believe God will honor who you are? God longs for us to accept his words of love. When we know how valuable we are to him, we have no need to pretend. We are free to love others genuinely.

THOUGHT

When have you tried to deceive someone else because you didn't believe that who you really are would be good enough?

Positively Honest

An honest answer is like a kiss on the lips.
—PROVERBS 24:26

One of my personal struggles with honesty has been how to respond to people who ask me to read their book manuscripts. Years ago, I would accept a manuscript, and it would lie on my desk for months. When I did read it, if it had a wholesome message, I would give encouraging feedback. Since I'm not an editor, I didn't comment on the quality of the writing. The writer would then attempt, without success, to get the manuscript published. Over time, I realized I was setting people up for disappointment.

Now when I am asked to read a manuscript, I say, "I am not good in assessing the value of a manuscript, nor does my schedule allow the time. I'd suggest that you ask an English teacher to read it for grammar and sentence structure and to make suggestions. Then submit it to a literary agency and see if they think it's worthy of publication." I offer useful advice while being honest about the limitations of my time and abilities.

When we are aware of who God made us to be, we won't try to be someone we're not. A part of being honest is acknowledging our limitations so we can give our attention to the tasks God calls us to.

PRAYER

Father, I pray for wisdom in knowing how to be honest about my limitations as well as my strengths.

Freewriting

The things that come out of the
mouth come from the heart.
—MATTHEW 15:18

Writing instructors sometimes assign a period of
"freewriting." That means writing down anything
that comes to mind without lifting the pen from paper and
without thinking about punctuation, grammar, or even meaning. Sometimes such an exercise helps people realize their
feelings about a situation or event because they write without
analyzing their thoughts.

It's a gift when we experience that kind of freedom in a
relationship, speaking honestly about our emotions, fears, and
hopes. Novelist Dinah Craik once wrote, "Oh, the comfort—
the inexpressible comfort of feeling *safe* with a person—

having neither to weigh thoughts nor measure words, but pouring them all right out, just as they are, chaff and grain together; certain that a faithful hand will take and sift them, keep what is worth keeping, and then with the breath of kindness blow the rest away."

This type of friendship is earned over time as two people come to trust each other. We might be honest in all our relationships but only completely open in one or two rare friendships. When we build trust with someone through consistent actions, truth in everything, and a willingness to speak difficult realities in a spirit of love, we enjoy the reward of a friendship that reflects the freedom we have with Christ.

PRAYER

Father, thank you that I can pour out
all my thoughts and feelings to you.
I pray for a close friend or friends with
whom I can share freely as well.

The Voice of Jesus

His sheep follow him because they
know his voice.

—JOHN 10:4

Author and poet Luci Shaw was looking for a campsite
in the Canadian Rockies when she noticed a deer
standing alone on the bank of a river. "She turned her head
toward me," Shaw writes, "and 'saw' me with her ears. When
I think of someone who listens sensitively for God and hears
him, I see in my mind this deer, on the alert for the slightest
sound or scent."

When we strive to make truth a part of our lives, our ears
will be attentive to God's voice alone. When Jesus stood
before Pilate, he said, "For this reason I was born, and for this

I came into the world, to testify to the truth. Everyone on the side of truth listens to me" (John 18:37).

As we actively seek out the truth, we will become more alert to the voice of Jesus. Every time we choose to hear and speak truth instead of falsehood, his voice becomes clearer to our souls.

PRAYER

Lord, I want to hear your wise and loving voice above all. Train my ears with the truth.

Honest to God

How is it that Satan has so filled your
heart that you have lied to the Holy Spirit?
—ACTS 5:3

A church with a heart for the poor held a pledge campaign to raise money for people in their community. Church members were generous, making large and sacrificial pledges of money.

One couple made an especially generous pledge, but when the time came to write the check, their pledge seemed too extravagant. Privately, they agreed to donate a smaller sum. The following Sunday after the offering was taken, the pastor noticed that the couple's check was smaller than he remembered their pledge to be.

"Is this what you pledged?" he asked them.

"Oh yes," they assured him. And then they dropped dead.

This might sound implausible, but something very similar to this happened in the time of the apostles when Ananias and Sapphira shortchanged a pledge they made to the Jerusalem church. The issue wasn't that God needed the extra drachmas; it was that the couple was dishonest before God. As the apostle Peter said to Ananias, "You have not lied to men but to God" (Acts 5:4).

Lying damages a relationship. If you have been tempted to lie to God, ask yourself why you feel the need to hide the truth. Speaking the truth to God not only strengthens your relationship with him but also prepares you for trustworthy relationships with others.

PRAYER

Lord, I want to be completely honest with you—about my sin, my feelings, my doubts, and my joys.

Inner Truth

Be made new in the attitude of your minds.
—EPHESIANS 4:23

Brooke never considered the books she read to be harmful. Reading Jane Austen's works or Christian romance novels seemed like a relaxing way to spend an evening.

But soon it became easy to picture herself in the scenes of the book. She started to compare men she dated to Mr. Darcy from *Pride and Prejudice* (they fell short) and to take innocent scenes from novels several steps further in her mind. She began to compromise her personal standards in order to live out the relational fantasies she'd been entertaining.

Then, sitting in church one Sunday, Brooke heard the pastor say, "Speaking the truth in love begins with speaking the truth to ourselves." The first thing that came to mind was the stack of romance novels on her nightstand. She had been lying to herself about the impact they had on her life. Lust and impossible standards had affected her relationships with men. The only way to change the pattern was to be honest with herself about her destructive reading habits.

When we speak the truth to ourselves, we are doing what leads to the best, most God-honoring lives and preparing our souls to love others.

THOUGHT

*In what areas of your life might
you be lying to yourself?*

No Offense?

Watch out for false prophets. They
come to you in sheep's clothing, but
inwardly they are ferocious wolves.
—MATTHEW 7:15

A round three hundred years after Christ, a new theory
called Arianism was circulating in the church, propa-
gating the belief that Jesus was not God in human flesh but
merely the highest of God's creations. Many leaders in the
early church were prepared to adopt this error, but Athanasius of Alexandria insisted that the church hold to the truth:
Jesus is God. This made Athanasius appear to be a trouble-
maker, and he was banished from Alexandria five times by different emperors. But in the end he established the orthodoxy

of the deity of Christ, and the church adopted a position that left no room for Arianism.

Was Athanasius being unloving because he made people angry? Quite the opposite. Love does not sit idly by while lives are destroyed by false teachings. But that kind of love can appear to be unloving to a world that looks at things through a distorted lens. As Dorothy Sayers wrote in *Letters to a Diminished Church,* "I believe it to be a grave mistake to present Christianity as something charming and popular with no offense in it."

Jesus's love led him to confront error with truth, even when to do so offended people. His respect for truthfulness serves as the perfect model for Christians who want to make love a way of life.

ACTION STEP

Think about what it takes to stand for truth when others prefer distortion and falsehood. Determine that you will speak the truth in love, even if you are the only one doing so.

Part 9

MAKING LOVE A WAY
OF LIFE EVERY DAY

In Christ's Strength

> I can do all things through Christ who
> strengthens me.
> —PHILIPPIANS 4:13, NKJV

Bookstore shelves are crowded with advice on how to break bad habits. Follow these eight steps. Wear this motivational wristband. Go to a hypnotist. Hire a personal trainer.

Specific techniques might help you break certain habits—it doesn't hurt to count to ten before speaking when you're upset, for instance. But the only way to make loving people a habit that flows naturally from your soul is through God's power.

To become a more loving person, you need to acknowledge to yourself and to God that you fall into unloving habits and you want to change. Be as specific as possible when you pray. Does your husband's tendency to leave muddy shoes on the carpet bring out your impatience more than anything else? Are you so weary of a co-worker's rudeness that you struggle to speak kindly to her? Tell God what it is that most often causes you to fall into unloving patterns.

Paul's declaration that you can do all things through the strength of Christ offers hope when unloving habits overwhelm you. You can't win this battle through willpower; it is Christ in you who offers the strength you need to love others.

PRAYER

Father, I want to break unloving patterns
in my life. Specifically, I want to

_____ .

Amazing Grace

> By this all men will know that you are my
> disciples, if you love one another.
> —JOHN 13:35

In his book *What's So Amazing About Grace?* Philip Yancey tells the story of a prostitute who rented out her two-year-old daughter for sex and used the money to support her drug habit. When asked if she had thought about going to church for help, a look of "pure, naive shock…crossed her face. 'Church!' she cried. 'Why would I ever go there? I was already feeling terrible about myself. They'd just make me feel worse.' "

This woman speaks for many people who believe that Christianity is more concerned with criticism than with love. In truth, Christians are called to lead the way in love. When we are unkind, impatient, unforgiving, rude, proud, greedy, and dishonest, we lose more than an opportunity to know the joy of loving others. We lose an opportunity to express God's love. In fact, our behavior becomes a hurdle between others and God.

Many ill-treated people have said, "If that is what it means to be a Christian, then I don't want to be one." At the same time, others have said: "That person showed me love when I didn't deserve it. I want to find out why." What great opportunities we have to surprise others with a spirit of servanthood! Only when we love with the love of God can we bring hope to an otherwise hopeless world.

PRAYER

Lord, thank you for the opportunity to show love to others. Help me to be a channel of your love so that others want to know you.

"Most of All"

[I] will continue to make you known in
order that the love you have for me may
be in them and that I myself may be in
them.

(JESUS PRAYING FOR ALL BELIEVERS)
—JOHN 17:26

Growing up, Mary Beth knew her parents loved her, but they were restrained in showing their love. She fondly remembers her childhood bedtime routine, because then she heard their love most clearly. Every night as her mother tucked her in bed she told Mary Beth, "Always remember: Mommy loves you. Daddy loves you. And Jesus loves you most of all."

Now Mary Beth is grown and her mother's spirited personality has faded under the ravages of Alzheimer's. As Mary Beth and her father care for her mom, Mary Beth holds her mother's hands and echoes the words her mom said to her years ago: "Always remember: I love you. Dad loves you. And Jesus loves you most of all."

Mary Beth doesn't know how much her mother understands. She does know that these simple words speak to her own heart because they remind her that God's love in us is powerful no matter how we feel. Our love is incomplete, but we keep loving people, knowing that Jesus is at work through us to show others the love of our heavenly Father.

It is God who loves us more than we can imagine. It is God who gives us the desire to love others extravagantly. And it is God who reminds us that Christ's unfailing love in us is what matters—most of all.

PRAYER

Father, help me understand your love so deeply that I can show it more freely.

Conclusion

Loving others comes as a result of drawing near to God. I hope that your journey through this book has helped you do that. The question now becomes, "Where do I go from here? How do I continue the journey of love?" Let me suggest that you continue in the way you have started—drinking deeply from the fountain of God's love. With that in mind, I want to suggest three simple practices that have sustained many Christians through the years.

First, set aside time every day to listen to God's voice. What I have found most helpful is to read a chapter in the Bible after saying this prayer: "Father, I'm listening to you. I want to hear what you have to say to me." As you read the chapter, underline the phrases or statements that particularly resonate with you. Then talk to God about the things you have underlined. This is a practical way to have a daily conversation with God. After all, your relationship with God is a love relationship. He initiated the process; you reciprocate by listening to and communicating with him.

Second, ask God daily to pour his love into your heart and to allow you to be a channel of his love flowing to others. Ask him to show you opportunities where you can express kindness, patience, forgiveness, courtesy, humility, generosity, and honesty.

Third, commit yourself to being a person of integrity, someone who doesn't let personal failures become barriers between you and others. Ask God to give you the courage to apologize when you have offended others. You need not be perfect to be a reflection of God's love, but you must deal effectively with your weaknesses.

In addition to these three practices, I suggest you continue to look for ways you can join other Christians in worshiping God, encouraging one another, and exploring how together you can serve God by serving others. We were designed to live in community with other members of the body of Christ. We have much to give and much to receive from other Christians.

When Christ returns, he is not going to ask how many Bible studies we attended or how many Scripture verses we memorized. His question will be, "How well did you represent me?" Most of the accomplishments that humans honor as things of greatness will one day be forgotten. But love will follow us into eternity. In a world gone mad with greed and hate, how wonderful to know a love that never ends—and what a privilege to be able to show that love to other people every day.

Notes

Please note that all Internet addresses were active and appropriate at the time of the writing of this book. I regret that I cannot guarantee their availability or content beyond that time.

Part 1: Love as a New Way of Life

5   Margaret Nelson and Keri Pickett, *Saving Body and Soul* (Colorado Springs, CO: Shaw, 2004), 75, 29, 27, 75.

Part 2: Kindness

21   Associated Press, "Study: Babies Can Tell Helpful, Hurtful Playmates," CNN.com, November 21, 2007, www.cnn.com/2007/HEALTH/11/21/infant.judging.ap/index.html.

25   Jenny Friedman, *The Busy Family's Guide to Volunteering* (Beltsville, MD: Robins Lane, 2003), 13.

27   C. S. Lewis, *Letters to an American Lady* (Grand Rapids, MI: Eerdmans, 1978), 108.

31   Jenna Glatzer, "A Girl's Home Is Her Castle," in *Stories of Strength,* ed. Jenna Glatzer (Morrisville, NC: Lulu.com, 2005), 172–73.

Part 3: Patience

41   Michael Kahn, "A Bad Relationship Can Cause Heart Attack: Study," Reuters, October 7, 2007, www.reuters.com/article/healthNews/idUSL0824271720071008.

44   Quotations from Jack Canfield and Mark Victor Hansen, comps., *A Third Serving of Chicken Soup for the Soul* (Deerfield Beach, FL: Health Communications, 1996), 275.

47   Ruth Bell Graham, *An Extraordinary Life* (Nashville: W Publishing, 2003), 173.

51   Eugene Peterson, *Earth and Altar* (Downers Grove, IL: InterVarsity, 1985), 78.

53   Don Fields, "Forty Years of Prayer," *Finding God Between a Rock and a Hard Place,* comp. Lil Copan and Elisa Fryling, (Wheaton, IL.: Harold Shaw, 1999), 36–38.

58   Frederick William Faber, *Growth in Holiness* (London: Thomas Richardson, 1860), 151.

Part 4: Forgiveness

63   Immaculée Ilibagiza, *Left to Tell* (Carlsbad, CA: Hay House, 2006), 203–4.

69   Fyodor Dostoevsky, *The Brothers Karamazov,* www.bibliomania.com/0/0/235/1030/frameset.html.

75   Linda Strom, *Karla Faye Tucker Set Free* (Colorado Springs, CO: Shaw Books, 2000), 49.

77   Jane Stuart Smith and Betty Carlson, *Great Christian Hymn Writers* (Wheaton, IL: Crossway, 1997), 164.

79 Henri Nouwen, *Here and Now* (New York: Crossroad, 1994),
    60.

81 Colin Moynihan, "Goodbye to Bad Memories, or Old Electric
    Bills," *New York Times,* December 29, 2007, www.nytimes
    .com/2007/12/29/nyregion/29shred.html. Also, see "New York-
    ers Shred Bad Memories of 2007," IOL, December 31, 2007,
    www.iol.co.za/index.php?set_id=1&click_id=29&art_id=nw20
    071231135802918C482393. Also, see New York Associated
    Press, "Shred Your Bad Memories of 2007," 2News, December
    19, 2007, www.2news.tv/green/greennational/12631611.html.

85 Associated Press, "Infamous Boston Jail Now a Luxury Hotel,"
    MSNBC, November 7, 2007, www.msnbc.msn.com/id/
    21676139. See also www.libertyhotel.com.

Part 5: Courtesy

91 Mother Teresa, *In My Own Words,* comp. José Luis González-
    Balado (Ligouri, MO: G. K. Hall and Liguori, 1996), 69.

93 Quotes and information taken from "The Martyrdom of Saint
    Polycarp, Bishop of Smyrna, as Told in the Letter of the
    Church of Smyrna to the Church of Philomelium," found in
    multiple sources, including Christian Classics Ethereal Library,
    www.ccel.org/ccel/richardson/fathers.vii.i.iii.html.

95 C. S. Lewis, *The Weight of Glory* (New York: Macmillan,
    1949), 19.

97 Margaret T. Jensen, *First We Have Coffee* (San Bernardino, CA:
    Here's Life, 1982), 110.

101 This anecdote from Gandhi's life can be found in numerous sources, including http://jmm.aaa.net.au/articles/552.htm.

105 A&E Television Network, *The Greatest Presidential Stories Never Told* (New York: HarperCollins, 2007), 20.

109 Ric Kahn, "Politeness Pleas," Boston Globe, December 23, 2007, www.boston.com/news/local/massachusetts/articles/2007/12/23/politeness_pleas/?rss_id=Boston.com+—+Massachusetts+news.

111 For more background on this story, see Geoffrey Hanks and Christian Herald, *Seventy Great Christians* (Scotland: Christian Focus, 2003), 260. Also, see http://en.wikipedia.org/wiki/Dwight_L._Moody.

Part 6: Humility

117 Miriam Huffman Rockness, *A Passion for the Impossible* (Wheaton, IL: Harold Shaw, 1999), 190.

119 Mark Galli and Ted Olsen, eds., *131 Christians Everyone Should Know* (Nashville: Broadman & Holman, 2000), 206.

125 For more information about Friedrich Nietzsche, see Catholic Education Resource Center at www.catholiceducation.org/articles/civilization/cc0009.html.

127 Kim Bolton with Chris Wave, "Da Big Chair," in *Finding God Between a Rock and a Hard Place,* comp. Copan and Fryling, 134–36.

129 Mrs. Howard Taylor, *Borden of Yale '09* (Philadelphia: China Inland Mission, 1927), 275.

132 Warren Wiersbe, quoted in George Sweeting, *Who Said That?* (Chicago: Moody, 1994), 369.

135 Cornelia Lehn, *Peace Be with You* (Newton, KS: Faith and Life, 1980), 91.

137 Robert Goodwin, Thomas Kinkade, and Pam Proctor, *Points of Light* (New York: Warner, 2006), 8.

Part 7: Generosity

141 William Garden Blaikie, *The Personal Life of David Livingstone* (Chestnut Hill, MA: Adamant Media, 2005), 139.

149 Oren Yaniv and Leo Standora, "Courageous Final Act of Professor," *New York Daily News,* April 17, 2007, www.nydailynews.com/news/ny_crime/2007/04/17/2007-04-17_courageous_final_act_of_professor.html.

151 John Bunyan, *The Pilgrim's Progress,* text available online at http://books.google.com/books?id=yNgGAAAAYAAJ&pg=PA220&lpg=PA220&dq=there+was+a+man+though+some+did+count+him+mad&source=web&ots=7wnjyTbwGi&sig=Qf51ghvhjoObMMirrt8WCgngzCI.

156 For more information about this church, see www.churchatrockcreek.org.

163 Sebastian Junger, "Sebastian Junger: Welcome Stranger," *National Geographic Adventure,* www.nationalgeographic.com/adventure/0605/features/sebastian_junger.html.

Part 8: Honesty

167 Daniel Taylor, *Letters to My Children* (Downers Grove, IL: InterVarsity, 1989), 96–97.

171 Jennifer Riley, "Analysis: Why Muslims Follow Jesus," *Christian Post Reporter,* November 16, 2007, www.christianpost .com/article/20071116/30110.htm.

173 "Caution: This Office Is a Gossip-Free Zone," *Good Morning, America,* November 13, 2007, http://abcnews.go.com/GMA/ WaterCooler/Story?id=3857737&page=1.

175 Steven D. Levitt and Stephen J. Dubner, *Freakonomics,* rev. ed. (New York: William Morrow, 2006), 239.

178 M. Craig Barnes, *Hustling God* (Grand Rapids, MI: Zondervan, 1999), 34.

181 This quote was originally published in 1859 in *A Life for a Life,* by Dinah Craik. Book text is available online at www3 .shropshire-cc.gov.uk/etexts/E000329.htm.

183 Luci Shaw, *Horizons* (Grand Rapids, MI: Zondervan, 1992), 40.

Part 9: Making Love a Way of Life Every Day

195 Philip Yancey, *What's So Amazing About Grace?* (Grand Rapids, MI: Zondervan, 1997), 11.

REDISCOVER
the power of love

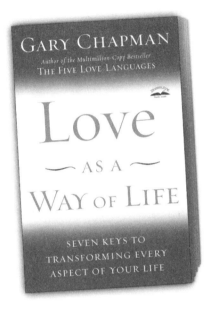

Why settle for less than the best in any of your relationships? In *Love As a Way of Life*, you'll learn about the seven essential habits that transform everyday encounters at work, at home, and in every area of your life.

Discussion guide included for individual or group study.
Also available in audio format.
Available in stores and from online retailers.

WATERBROOK PRESS
www.waterbrookpress.com